Implementing Restorative Practices in Schools

D1514104

of related interest

Just Schools
A Whole School Approach to Restorative Justice
Belinda Hopkins
Foreword by Guy Masters
ISBN 987 1 84310 132 1
eISBN 978 1 84642 432 8

Just Care
Restorative Justice Approaches to Working with Children in Public Care
Belinda Hopkins
Foreword by Jonathan Stanley
ISBN 978 1 84310 981 5
eISBN 978 0 85700 087 3

Cyberbullying and E-safety
What Educators and Other Professionals Need to Know
Adrienne Katz
ISBN 978 1 84905 276 4
eISBN 978 0 85700 575 5

E-Safety for the i-Generation
Combating the Misuse and Abuse of Technology in Schools
Nikki Giant
ISBN 978 1 84905 944 2
eISBN 978 0 85700 774 2

Self-Esteem Games for Children
Deborah M. Plummer
Illustrated by Jane Serrurier
£15.99/$29.95 (paperback)
ISBN 978 1 84310 424 7
eISBN 978 1 84642 574 5

Equipping Young People to Choose Non-Violence
A Violence Reduction Programme to Understand Violence, Its Effects, Where it Comes From and How to Prevent It
Gerry Heery
ISBN 978 1 84905 265 8
eISBN 978 0 85700 605 9

Implementing Restorative Practices in Schools

A Practical Guide to Transforming School Communities

Margaret Thorsborne and Peta Blood
Foreword by Graham Robb

Jessica Kingsley *Publishers*
London and Philadelphia

First published in 2013
by Jessica Kingsley Publishers
73 Collier Street
London N1 9BE, UK
and
400 Market Street, Suite 400
Philadelphia, PA 19106, USA

www.jkp.com

Copyright © Margaret Thorsborne and Peta Blood 2013
Foreword copyright © Graham Robb 2013

All rights reserved. No part of this publication may be reproduced in any material
form (including photocopying or storing it in any medium by electronic means and
whether or not transiently or incidentally to some other use of this publication)
without the written permission of the copyright owner except in accordance with the
provisions of the Copyright, Designs and Patents Act 1988 or under the terms of a
licence issued by the Copyright Licensing Agency Ltd, Saffron House, 6–10 Kirby
Street, London EC1N 8TS. Applications for the copyright owner's written permission
to reproduce any part of this publication should be addressed to the publisher.

Warning: The doing of an unauthorised act in relation to a copyright work may result
in both a civil claim for damages and criminal prosecution.

Library of Congress Cataloging in Publication Data
Thorsborne, Margaret.
  Implementing restorative practice in schools : a practical guide to transforming
school communities /
Margaret Thorsborne and Peta Blood ; foreword by Graham Robb.
     pages cm
  Includes bibliographical references.
  ISBN 978-1-84905-377-8 (alk. paper)
  1. Problem children--Education. 2. Problem children--Behavior modification. I.
Blood, Peta. II. Title.
  LC4801.T56 2013
  371.93--dc23
                              2013010146

British Library Cataloguing in Publication Data
A CIP catalogue record for this book is available from the British Library

ISBN 978 1 84905 377 8
eISBN 978 0 85700 737 7

Printed and bound in Great Britain by Bell & Bain Ltd, Glasgow

Contents

Foreword

If only this book had been available when my school started on its restorative journey! Even then I kept coming across Marg and Peta and their inclusion of international perspectives wherever they were working. They are among that key group of practitioner–innovator and researchers working in and with schools as we share the ups and downs of becoming restorative.

At first it was restorative process that got many engaged – and that we were sharing and learning about. We asked how the principles could be applied in different settings and with different groups of young people:

- younger and older

- those with specific learning needs

- those causing more serious degrees of harm or even law breaking

- those in mainstream schools and those in units for children excluded from schools.

But it was also the way in which restorative process could work with adults (staff, families and communities) as much as with young people that caught our attention. This meant a focus on issues of school policy, governance and leadership and the goal of the Restorative School.

This book is a map for schools wherever they are on the restorative journey, and for staff at any level who exercise, aspire to or hold a leadership role. It sets out very clearly the 'Second Order Change' – deep change which inhabits the DNA of the school and which is needed in order for a school to become restorative – and, drawing on a wealth of evidence and experience, shows how staff from the early adopters to the laggards can be helped to reflect, learn and change even when that means 'fierce, honest restorative conversations'. It is also a reminder to leaders not to 'drop the wheelbarrow' once they have reached a shared milestone on the way to becoming a restorative school.

There are always new pupils or students, staff and local governance authorities, and they will continue to need to learn anew about being a restorative school. Crucially this book also puts restorative work in the context of schools' learning goals and shows, with data and stories, how a restorative school is one which is better able to support the aspirations we have for our children to succeed in their learning.

This is a map for single schools and for groups of schools that are determined to be a restorative school system serving a particular area. This is a different scale of operation, but the same principles and practice apply as for a single school, with additional opportunities for sharing, support, challenge and engagement.

One of the stages on my school's restorative journey was to create a new slogan. I am still proud that our collective efforts as a school community working through our restorative journey produced 'Learning Together to Succeed', which I think encapsulates the collective, collaborative, continual and above all relational learning which is at the heart of a restorative school.

Marg and Peta have done a huge favour to schools by distilling their years of training, research, reflection and leadership in this eminently practical but also inspirational book. Wherever you are on your restorative school journey, this book will help.

Graham Robb
Former secondary school headteacher
who works in education and youth justice fields,
chair of the Restorative Justice Council in the UK

Acknowledgements

No part of this book would have been possible without the quiet and patient support of our loved ones, Jan and Mick, who besides having to read our words, offer advice, make corrections and supply many cups of tea, have had to cope with the days, weeks and months of having us immersed in something other than family. Not to mention the sacrifices they have made while we have dedicated ourselves over many years to the pursuit of what works best in this fascinating and life-giving field of restorative practice. Thank you both from the bottom of our hearts.

We would like to extend our appreciation to fellow consultants in the fields of leadership development and change management. In particular, our close colleague Sharon Borrows of Growth Dynamics, Australia, has helped us to broaden our understanding of how these two vital pieces connect with restorative practice; her contributions can be felt in Sections 2 and 3 of this book.

We want to acknowledge the important work of practitioners in this relatively new field of restorative practice in schools who continue to astound us with their passion, dedication and innovation and their contributions to our collective wisdom. In our own early days, we would never have dreamt of the possibilities that are now emerging. As pioneers, we are now becoming students of these people, learning from them as they continue to develop practice, and that is how it should be. We are also indebted to the academic world that provides us with the valuable research that allows us to know what works, and why it works.

We would like to honour and thank our colleagues – the change agents who work as consultants as we do, and those who work inside our government departments and other organisations, including schools. We appreciate the sharing and the collaborative nature of these relationships, knowing that together we will make a difference. The world is changing so fast that we must remember what really matters if we want to raise young people to be the best they can be, that they are responsible, accountable, kind, caring, compassionate, thoughtful and mindful of others. In the end, it's all about relationships.

Introduction

It's likely that you've picked up this book to read because you are interested in introducing the restorative philosophy to the way behaviour is managed in your school and because you want young people behaving more appropriately. Or you feel the progress of your implementation has stalled. Or you simply want to know if you are on track. We'd like you to think bigger than this. We'd like you to picture the whole school community committed to the pursuit of best practice in teaching and learning and how that whole pursuit is vitally connected to the quality of relationships in the classroom and beyond. We'd like to think about the way all relationships in the school can be transformed, not just what needs to happen when a student does the wrong thing.

What we write about is how to think about and manage large-scale change in the way everyone thinks and behaves – in other words, changing the culture in your school. We both know from bitter experience the heartache, frustrations and disappointments involved in the failure of an organisation to recognise or embrace a good idea when they see one, despite our collective best efforts. We didn't know then what we know now about change. Best, then, that we help you understand this concept of culture change in greater depth, before setting about developing a reform strategy for your school.

Implementing restorative practice (RP) is about changing the hearts and minds of everyone so that they are focused on strengthening and repairing relationships in their classrooms and across the school community. The focus also needs to be about how we prevent problems from occurring in the first instance and what we need to do to ensure this practice and that our policies support it. That when a situation continues to occur we are inquisitive and concerned about what needs to happen, rather than blaming the child, the parent or the teacher. That problems are our problems, rather than that problem child, that class, that teacher or that school.

Until this occurs, restorative practice may be seen as little more than a tool used by staff in key behaviour management positions, but not something that is integrated into the daily practice of teaching and leading a school community.

The distinction is seeing restorative practice as part of 'the way we do things around here', versus something we use as an occasional tool when a child is in trouble. An effective restorative process may assist someone to think about his or her behaviour, and when done well, deal with the impact of that behaviour on others. We cannot expect any single restorative process to address broader issues that are impacting on behaviours in general. By this we mean broader issues around poor attitudes and skills of some teachers and middle managers; inadequate induction processes for staff, students and parents; or socio-economic circumstances of the student and family and the influence this has on behaviour. The school might not have a learning culture that is committed to using the latest research and best practice. A comment from a colleague over dinner recently was telling when they said that education, and its key decision-makers at region/county/state and national level, is one of the few professions that does not pursue, in the main, current research and best practice about what works and what doesn't. Many decisions are political and are made with a view to winning votes at the next election or made with a dominant view that social capital doesn't matter as much as economic capital. Imagine a surgeon *not* using the latest techniques to improve the outcomes of surgery for patients. Why is it that it takes so long to take up best practice? We hope our book can help you understand this and be better equipped to meet the challenges ahead.

The approach to implementation needs to be comprehensive and multi-faceted. For restorative practice to be successful, it is reliant on having a bed of healthy relationships. Otherwise, we must ask, 'What are we restoring to?' If healthy relationships do not exist, then it is highly unlikely that the implementation of restorative practice will achieve the types of results we know it can, including dramatically lowering suspensions, exclusions, referrals and detention rates, not to mention improvements in academic outcomes for students.

Enormous care must be taken to plan and manage the change process so that the job of culture change is achieved with a strengthening of relationships and social capital. It must be achieved with, not done to. While attention has to be given to aligning policy and practice, to changing structures and processes where necessary, we must realise that this is the 'easy' piece of work – the hard work is getting people's books open at the same page, aligning hearts and minds and values, challenging prevailing beliefs about the most effective way to raise young people and to change behaviour. This is deeply emotional work, and people's responses will vary from enthusiasm and excitement, through a wait-and-see attitude, to scepticism and downright resistance, both overt and covert. This is something we talk about in much more detail later in this book. Change has to start with the adults in a school community. As professionals in the school community, we must be held accountable for our practice and, in Mahatma Ghandi's (1913) paraphrased words, we must be the change we want to see in the world (as cited in Government of India 1999). If the adults in the school do not use the restorative language and do not model restorative behaviours, then how can we expect students to do so?

The title of this book was chosen to indicate that we need to be clear about the possibilities of transformative change in your school – a change process that becomes evident when staff return to work in the school some years later and say in astonishment, 'I can't believe how different it is now. How settled and calm the kids are these days.' While there are a number of useful texts on the market about restorative practice and how to 'do' it, with some guidelines for implementation, we consider that this book takes a deeper view of change that is reflected in Sections 2 and 3.

What's in this Book and What Isn't

It will be helpful if we tell you what is and isn't included in our book. And we'll start with what isn't. You will not find instructions on how to facilitate restorative processes in your school or classrooms. You will not find instructions about how to facilitate circles or class meetings where relationships are developed and social and emotional competencies built. You will not find lesson plans for developing these competencies. You will not find instructions about how to manage restorative performance conversations with individual staff, or how to facilitate workplace conferences or circles for teams and faculties that might need some restoring. There are plenty of books and manuals to do that and some of these we recommend to you in our Further Reading section.

What you will find is divided into three distinct sections. The first section, A Whole School Approach, is written for those of you just beginning your journey with restorative practice. We explain the theory and philosophy of restorative justice and how schools have adapted it into a continuum of practice to cover a range of situations: some serious, some minor and those in between. We discuss the issue of punishment and whether or not it delivers what we need it to deliver to maximise learning. We explore 'layers' of practice to be put in place in order to have a comprehensive whole school approach, including the preventive work that needs to be done to create a positive culture and base for this work in the first place. And we have made some important links between RP and its positive impact on the relationship between teachers and learners and classroom climate for learning. We examine the issue of social and emotional competence and their links to learning, and how RP can help develop these vital life skills in both adults and young people, and how important they are to have for participating in this approach to problem-solving. The final part of this section is devoted to thinking about what a school that is truly restorative might look like, sound like, feel like.

Section 2, Managing the Change Process, is included because, unless practitioners are already in senior positions in a school engaged in a large-scale change process or doing further study around educational leadership, it is unlikely that they have had an opportunity to understand the issues around organisational change and its complexities. We have included some helpful insights into the reasons why people may not share our enthusiasm for RP, and how to work with them to overcome their anxieties, cynicism and resistance. This means we have to understand the emotional impact of change on people and how to work with these strong emotions to minimise the negativity and maximise interest and enjoyment – to bring people along with us. We need to know what sort of change we need in order to bring about the kind of outcomes we are after; how deep the change has to be to be effective; and what makes a change process effective or ineffective. And last, but definitely not least, we have included some material on leadership. From our own experiences working in schools undergoing change of this nature we have found that the style and strength of school leadership, how relational it is, and the way leadership is encouraged in others, will make or break the implementation efforts of great practitioners.

Section 3, Making It Happen: An Implementation Guide, will take you through eight practical steps that will help you get to the kind of place and culture (the way we do things around here) that you and your team might have envisaged. These eight steps are built mainly around the work of John Kotter, a change management expert, and others, and we are deeply grateful for the access we have had to their thinking and materials. These concrete steps, together with the supporting material found in the appendices will allow you and your team to be less random, more strategic – and altogether more effective – in working through the complexities of changing paradigms with your staff, students and parents, so that the culture you want sticks.

Terminology

Throughout the book you will read references to the term restorative practice (RP). In other places in our now-international community, you might be using terms such as restorative measures, or restorative approaches or restorative interventions, or others. If you need to, please make the translation in your own head to the familiar terms you use in your country, state or county. We mean the same. And in recognition of differences in other terminology, you might find us using senior leadership or senior management teams (SLT or SMT). Your preference might be senior administration teams (SAT). What we mean of course, again, is the same thing. There might be other points of difference. Down Under we speak about students. You might call them pupils. We might speak of principals. You might refer to them as head teachers. You might use the term suspension, whilst others refer to this as fixed-term exclusion or stand-down. We hope you can read our work without being distracted by what we believe are minute differences. Schools are much the same wherever they are, and the issues teachers, leaders and young people and their families face are universal.

We would love to think you might contact us with your stories or corrections or questions, or give us some valuable feedback about whether or not you found this book useful. This journey into the restorative philosophy and how it translates into the educational setting is still a new one, and we both think that we are learning with you. If we have learnt anything at all about this journey, it is that we learn best together.

A Whole School Approach

Chapter 1

Restorative Practice Explained

Successful implementation of restorative practice in schools requires a firm understanding of the philosophy and the nature of this practice. This includes an understanding of what can be achieved, what can get in the way, and how to bring people on board in a strategic rather than a haphazard way. Starting with the end in mind, we consider what it is to be a restorative school and how to build the case for change.

In Section 1 we answer two critical questions:

- Why would a school adopt restorative practice?

- What is the relationship between restorative practice and quality teaching and learning?

In answering these fundamental questions, we address:

- what we mean by restorative practice

- how restorative practice is integral to the core business of teaching and learning

- how restorative practice enhances social and emotional literacy, and

- the difference this can make to a school community in terms of staff relationships with one another, with parents and with students.

We begin by exploring the notion of restorative justice, how it relates to the dominant retributive justice paradigm still present in criminal justice, in many schools, families, organisations and the wider community, and the challenges this poses if we want to change how we do things in schools. We need to understand the limitations of punishment in the achievement of compliance, or more importantly, in achieving the climate that supports learning in classrooms and the development of social and emotional competence in our young people.

Restorative practice (RP), or as it is known elsewhere, restorative measures (RM) or restorative approaches (RA), in schools has been in developmental mode since the mid-nineties, and remains so, as practitioners find more ways to apply the principles in different settings and situations. In Section 1 we look at the range of restorative practices as we explore the continuum of practice, and we will also explain a whole school model that explores not just these restorative responses, but what a school could be doing in terms of developing a healthy school environment that is conducive to learning. We will make links between RP and how it will enhance the core business of the school – that is, pedagogy (teaching and learning in classrooms). We will explore how RP can help with the deliberate development of the values, attitudes and skills for students, staff, management and families, so that working together in this way will become the glue that holds everything together.

We conclude Section 1 with what a restorative school might look like, feel like and sound like, so you can get a sense of the end point you might be working towards.

In a nutshell, restorative practice (RP/RM/RA) is the *practice* of restorative justice (RJ), a philosophical approach to crime and wrongdoing that puts harm done, accountability for that harm by the wrongdoer, and repair of that harm at the centre of the problem-solving, involving the stakeholders in the matter. Initiated in the 1970s in Ontario, Canada, and later in Indiana, USA, in Mennonite communities (Zehr 2002), modern RJ was a way of assisting offenders to take responsibility for their actions by helping them to understand and to repair the harm done to victims and their families. Starting with victim–offender mediation, practice has been prolific and varied, dependent on the culture, practice and ways of working already in place or developed as a result.

Restorative justice is a different paradigm, or mindset, from retributive justice. The two paradigms are illustrated in Table 1.1 adapted from Zehr (2002) where different sets of questions are asked in the wake of wrongdoing, whether in a criminal justice setting, a school, a workplace, a church, a family or a community.

Table 1.1 Two paradigms (adapted from Zehr 2002)

Retributive justice	Restorative justice
Crime and wrongdoing are violations against the laws/rules: what laws/rules have been broken?	Crime and wrongdoing is a violation of people and relationships: who has been harmed? In what way?
Blame must be apportioned: who did it?	Obligations must be recognised: Whose are these?
Punishment must be imposed: what do they deserve?	How can the harm be repaired?

In practice, retributive justice tends to isolate offenders/wrongdoers from any connection or problem-solving with those they have harmed, with the state or institution taking responsibility for decision-making about what punishment is to be imposed. With a restorative approach to problem-solving, those responsible and those harmed are together involved in dialogue that explores the event, the harm done, and together (within the legislative framework that might confine their decisions) work out a way forward. On the one hand, we have an approach that keeps people apart, indeed, *pushes* people apart; on the other hand, we have an approach that brings people together.

1.1 A Changing Paradigm in Schools

Over the years, we have each had the opportunity to work in many schools in different countries and education systems. Discipline, everywhere it seems, has had a history of being built on a solid foundation of retributive justice. It has been the norm, in the community, in families, in the justice system and before recent times hardly questioned except for the stories told by adults still bitter from their own experiences at school. If you did the wrong thing, you were punished. Even if you didn't do it, and people in authority thought you did, you still got what you 'deserved'. The 'story behind the story' was of no importance and often children were labelled as being naughty, bad, brats, etc. If you broke the rules, you were disobedient and you suffered the consequences.

Howard Zehr (2002) eloquently articulates the shift involved from this traditional punitive way of dealing with transgressions to a restorative approach. In a school setting these two approaches look quite different.

Retributive approach

In a traditional approach to school discipline, the enquiry is one of blame and punishment. We describe this as a quick fix, although there is ample research to demonstrate that it rarely leads to the required behaviour change, unless it involves the death penalty, an option thankfully denied to schools! In fact, it tends to give us more of what we are trying to eliminate. In a traditional, retributive approach, the enquiry is:

1. What school/classroom/playground rule was broken?

2. Who is to blame?

3. What punishment or sanction is deserved?

The usual forms of punitive consequences still being used in schools include sanctions such as:

1. removal from class to be sent to the disciplinarian's office

2. isolation in or outside of class

3. detention and detention plus (compound interest earned for not turning up the first time)

4. writing of lines

5. removal of privileges (e.g. you can no longer use the student common room)

6. not being allowed to go on a field trip or excursion

7. group punishment (e.g. the whole class on detention)

8. humiliation, belittling, name calling, use of sarcasm

9. suspension/stand-down/fixed-term exclusions

10. exclusion and or expulsion

11. yelling, shouting, growling, scolding

12. sending a young person to someone else to be 'fixed'

13. caning (still present in some countries where it has not yet been outlawed in legislation).

These strategies have two broad hoped-for outcomes: to inflict pain in order to act as a *deterrent* to the wrongdoer and others (and sometimes to serve the purpose of revenge if we are to be honest); and to *reduce re-offending*. They are only rarely successful at achieving these and are reliant on the young person's responsibility to self-correct and regulate their own behaviour, as the act itself does not bring about learning. In most instances it simply reinforces the internal story that *there is something wrong with me*, or *I hate this person for doing this to me*.

It is an approach that is arbitrary, about finding the right person to blame, and about a set of predetermined sanctions. There is minimal learning by the wrongdoer (or anyone else) and certainly no place for repairing the damage done. Wrongdoers are often labelled and, once they repeat their crime, find it difficult to shed the label. Teachers and other students see this young person as the problem child. Unfortunately, the relationships of people involved are often damaged as a result of the action-taking by the school, since no attention is paid to the harm done to relationships in the first instance.

Restorative approach

A restorative approach, on the other hand, is a different enquiry, one that is much more focused on relationships and repairing of harm. In our adaptation of Zehr's (2002) work, this translates to:

1. What happened?

2. Who has been harmed? How?

3. What needs to happen to repair the harm?

A restorative approach is relational and anything but a 'one size fits all', prescriptive approach to problem-solving. With this approach, there is an understanding that when wrong is done, we need to work with those involved to help them take responsibility for their behaviour, to learn from the incident and to take what action is required to repair the harm. It is necessary to pay attention to the stories of those harmed, in order to repair the harm, and to help the person responsible understand how their actions have affected others.

Howard Zehr (2002) advises that the three pillars of restorative justice — *harm, obligations*, and *engagement and participation* — must be evident for a successful restorative approach. We summarise Zehr's (2002) explanation of each:

- *Harm.* Justice begins with a focus on victims and their needs; it seeks to repair the harm in ways that are substantive as well as symbolic. This view of harm also extends to harm suffered by wrongdoers and the wider community.

- *Obligations.* Recognition of obligations places an emphasis on wrongdoer accountability and responsibility. This means the wrongdoer must be helped to understand the consequences *for others* of their behaviour, and they have a responsibility to make things right as far as it is possible, both substantively and symbolically. The community also bears responsibilities and accountabilities.

- *Engagement and participation.* Inclusion of the key people involved in what happened is important. Participants are involved in the process of telling the story of what happened, exploring the harm, and making decisions about how to resolve the issues. In its purest form, this is a level playing field, with all parties having equal space to tell their stories, to be understood, to have their wrongs righted.

If any of these three pillars are missing, then we have to question whether our approach has been restorative. Simply sending a student out of the classroom to be 'disciplined' by another staff member who has a slightly restorative dialogue *may* result in some awareness and understanding by the student about their responsibility but it rarely attends to the needs of those impacted by the behaviour and certainly fails on the engagement level. In this way, it is little more than a punitive approach to discipline that has a mild restorative flavour to it.

1.2 The Problem with Punishment

There is a plethora of convincing studies emerging that demonstrate that punishment is counterproductive to creating a climate of healthy connectedness in a school community. Blum, McNeeley and Rinehart (2002) in their longitudinal study of connectedness among US school students found that harsh discipline contributes to a sense of disconnect in the school environment. The impact of this disconnect is that students who feel disconnected from their peers and their school are more likely to hurt themselves, hurt others and/or participate in risky and dangerous behaviours (Blum *et al.* 2002). Alfie Kohn (2006, p.28) suggests that the use of punishment actually impedes the process of ethical development with a focus of what will happen to the child ('this is what will happen to *you* if you persist in following this pathway'), rather than what the consequences will be for *others*. Other notable authors (Coloroso 2003; Grille 2005; Morrison 2007) agree that punishment used as a standard tool for the achievement of compliance no longer delivers the kind of hopeful outcomes that we dreamed possible, and that these methods are indeed counterproductive.

Howard Zehr (2007) points out a number of reasons why there are problems with punishment:

- There are risks that wrongdoers will simply become angry with those who punish them. Kohn (2000) makes the same point, stating that punishment (often guised as sanctions, negative incentives or consequences) 'creates a climate of fear, and fear generates anger and resentment' (p.97).

- The threat of punishment leads to denial of responsibility (pleading not guilty, outright lying), making excuses, and minimising the harm (they can afford it, it didn't hurt anyone).

- The capacity to empathise with the victim is not encouraged if there is no process of coming together.

- Punishment doesn't get at the root causes, a point echoed by Kohn (2006).

Zehr (2002) also refers to noted violence expert James Gilligan (1997), who, in his book *Violence: Reflections on a National Epidemic,* suggests that all violence by a perpetrator, for example, is an effort to gain respect when s/he has felt disrespected. Zehr (2007) also noted in a plenary address with educators in Auckland, New Zealand, that a study of some 20,000 studies of punishment across justice, corrections, schools, families and communities showed that it did not produce the kinds of behaviour changes that were intended. Damning evidence to our thinking!

Ruby Payne (2009) in her ground-breaking work on understanding the values and behaviours of students and families who live in poverty, states:

> In poverty, discipline is about penance and forgiveness, not necessarily change. Because love is unconditional and because the timeframe is the present, the notion that discipline should be instructive and change behaviour is not part of the culture in generational poverty. (p.77)

In other words, if we want change, for these students who live in a different world from most middle class school values, we have to be prepared to teach them how to behave while they are at school, even if it is different from how they behave in their world.

By the time you are reading this, more discoveries in neuroscience (Brooks 2012; Doidge 2008; Lane and Garfield 2012; Lewis, Amini and Lannon 2001) will probably reinforce our recent understanding about why restorative processes are far more effective in delivering required behaviour change than traditional punitive sanctions. Le Messurier (2010) writes elegantly about the impact of poor 'executive functioning' in the prefrontal regions of the brain, which is vitally important to the kinds of concentration, tasks and behaviours we expect and need for the complex learning of today's classrooms. The Harvard University (2012) Center on the Developing Child refers to the impact of toxic stress on a child's development and wellbeing. Toxic stress 'occurs when a child experiences strong, frequent, and/or prolonged adversity – such as physical or emotional abuse, chronic neglect, caregiver substance abuse or mental illness, exposure to violence, and/or the accumulated burdens of family economic hardship – without adequate adult support' (Harvard University 2012, para. 6). Prolonged stress responses such as this can disrupt brain development, impact health and 'increase the risk for stress-related disease and cognitive impairment, well into the adult years' (Harvard University 2012, para. 6).

Punishment has a compounding effect on children who are already dealing with multiple stress and trauma in their lives. Punishment contributes to this stress, something that may be very evident in those children who are easily aroused and explode in anger and rage on being challenged about their behaviour. What we do know from the wonderful work of Doidge (2008) and other neuroplasticians is that the brain can change and, by creating new experiences (with focus and repetition), new brain pathways can be formed. We recommend that this new kind of knowledge about how brains work, especially in young people, be used to inform both our teaching practice and our management of behaviours and relationships in the classrooms – although in our minds, the two cannot be separated!

So one might wonder why such ineffective practices still exist. The lure of the quick fix is a siren call, and it takes enormously strong leadership at the head of education department/ministry level to turn around the impulse to demonise and label children, and look inwards to review paradigms and failing systems. All of this in the face of strong political pressure to legislate for increasingly harsher penalties, whether in schools or the criminal justice system – despite the knowledge that this does not work! Sometimes it is easy to despair in the face of such obstacles, but we are also reassured by the great work being done at the workface by committed teachers and school leaders who understand that the new sciences can contribute deeply to our understanding of what works best.

1.3 History of Restorative Practice in Schools

While building a case for using restorative, rather than retributive, approaches to problem-solving, we also need to know the story about how what was essentially a process that had its roots in criminal justice made its way into the school setting. Early elements of RJ can be found in countries in all parts of the world and as far back in history as written and spoken records go. What is clear is that the western world in particular seems to have lost the fine art of engaging in challenging dialogue, instead resorting to violence, litigation or complete avoidance. Of course, a breakdown in relationships and close community bonds has had much to do with this, particularly in the western world. It is far easier to hurt someone when the connection is weakened or not present, and we can afford to hide behind retributive processes when we are no longer accountable to one another in the community. Processes that we refer to as restorative were very evident in indigenous communities, especially before European colonisation. It was understood that to maintain community, they needed to deal with wrongdoing and have the challenging conversations. Not that all processes might pass the restorative test, nonetheless, they were effective for their time. It is therefore not surprising that modern educators and others who work with young people might have reached similar conclusions about the possibilities of how the principles of RJ might work in a school.

Before telling this particular story, however, we would like to acknowledge that the narrative about the transition of RJ into schools is likely to differ depending on the author and geography. We admit here quite openly that our story is biased in the matter of both authorship and geography, a 'Down Under' view, but that it by no means diminishes the extraordinary work done in other parts of the world (particularly in the northern hemisphere) by like-minded individuals who have responded to the call of the basic philosophy, values and possibilities of RJ.

In the early 1990s the Queensland (Australia) Department of Education was looking to develop a whole school approach to bullying. While the current literature and best practice models (Maines and Robinson 1994) seemed to solve our need for responses to low-to-medium level bullying, we were challenged by what to do about serious bullying. When we discovered a process called Community (Restorative) Conferencing, it sounded like an answer to our prayers. This process was being used by police in New South Wales (Australia) to divert young people away from court and seemed to offer the possibilities of more positive outcomes for all parties affected by an incident. It, in turn, had evolved from a youth justice process (the Family Group Conference) written into legislation in New Zealand in 1989 to better reflect the Maori cultural approach of problem-solving. The New Zealand process involved connecting with and involving family in decision-making about what to do in the wake of youth crime.

In the mid-1990s, the first trial of what was ostensibly a youth justice process was held in Queensland schools. The evaluation of that trial (Cameron and Thorsborne 2001) was very encouraging and the practice of conferencing for serious offences in schools quickly spread. Other Australian states followed suit with successful trials in New South Wales (McKenzie 1999) and Victoria (Shaw and Wierenga 2002). RP continues to be used in many schools worldwide for this purpose with the practice continuing to evolve.

One question that was asked during the evaluations of the conference process in Australia was whether or not its use for serious offences changed the culture of the school community. We were bothered in a naïve kind of way to discover that indeed it did not. Since this time, we have come to understand more about change management, and that it was entirely unrealistic to expect that an intervention to resolve a serious problem could transform a whole school community. For a number of reasons: the process didn't reach enough of the population of children and young people; and the philosophy and practice did not reach deep into the hearts and minds of enough staff in the school community to change their practice around matters of discipline or the ways in which they wielded their authority in classrooms or out in the yard or playground. Put simply, it made a tremendous difference to those involved in the process and certainly reduced the likelihood of the wrongdoers committing the same offence, but did not reach beyond this to touch the rest of the school community.

This early work coincided with a dawning understanding by some educators and researchers that merely removing a student in a suspension/fixed-term exclusion/stand-down for a serious (and often not-so-serious) offence failed in so many ways. Removal failed to satisfy those directly harmed and those affected in the wider school community. It failed to provide a real learning opportunity for the student responsible, or for the system to examine itself for its own failures. It failed to support deep behaviour change and it failed to provide the student with an opportunity for a fresh start and reintegration into their class or school community. It also discriminated against young people already marginalised in the school community (Skiba *et al.* 2003). So the time was ripe to begin questioning what on earth we were *doing* in schools with discipline and what it was we were trying to *achieve*.

At around the same time, the NSW Police Restorative Justice Unit (RJU) were working in a primary school in inner western Sydney, NSW, Australia, and a regional secondary school outside of Sydney, in Newcastle. The migration of their work from policing to schools was a natural one for them. The pathway to offending was very clear. That is, most *adult* offenders were *young* offenders, and most young offenders had a poor history of schooling. This meant that they were consistently under notice, sent from classrooms, on detention, suspended, excluded or had poor attendance consequently and were disengaged from learning. The work on connectedness clearly identifies the risk that prolonged absences, suspension and exclusion have on the students involved, placing them at high risk of hurting themselves, hurting others and participating in risky behaviour (Blum *et al.* 2002). Students who are disconnected from their peers and school are at high risk of falling foul of the law or hurting others. One only has to look at the school massacres perpetrated by a handful of students in the USA to see the pattern of disconnection involved in such tragic accounts.

Lewisham Primary School in the inner west of Sydney was a prime environment to test out a lot of this practice and theory. The school had a small population of 110 students, most of whom were new immigrants to the country, indigenous and/or from lower socio-economic groups. The diversity of culture and language in the school was incredible. The visionary principal knew that there was more that could be done and sought the assistance of many, including the Police RJU. The RP work started with whole school training by both the RJU and the Department of Education Itinerant Support Behaviour Team to ensure that practice could be developed across other schools without being reliant on an external group.

A key starting point was developing an understanding of what was happening in the school and exactly what students, teachers and parents were dealing with. From this, the approach focused on how to assist a largely transitory population to settle quickly and for children to transition well in and out of the school. Behavioural issues were understood in a context of the trauma and upheaval that came with many of the students and their families. Programmes were put in place to assist them in dealing with this and for their parents to connect with the available community support. It was through this early work that the layers of practice were expanded, and the restorative 'chat' or 'corridor conference', as we called it then, became the most visible practice. The continuum of restorative practice was extended, with a focus on the preventative/proactive end of the spectrum. The project also helped this school and many others since to re-think their entire approach to behaviour management. This aligned well with the work of Glaser (1969), Kohn (1996), Ahmed (1996; as cited in Ahmed *et al.* 2001) calling for a change in the way schools manage students. As Kohn (1996) aptly put it, are we *doing things to students* or *working with them?*

The work that followed in the Australian Capital Territory (ACT) in the late 1990s helped develop the firm understanding that RP had the ability to transform school cultures. This meant that embedding practice needed to be thought of as a *vehicle* for cultural change. It was clear that a school could not be restorative without substantial re-engineering of the way they did things, at a behaviour management and at a relational level. The ACT provided a fertile ground for the development of whole school practice, as consultants, academics and practitioners worked together to develop sustainable practice that supported schools in addressing the incidence of bullying, suspension, behavioural issues and exclusions. Ultimately the shift occurred in working with visionary school principals who saw the need to do things differently.

Chapter 2

Restorative Practice in Schools

When we write and speak about working restoratively in a school, with young people and each other, we describe working in a way that places value on the quality and health of relationships between the people involved in these interactions. It might be with the relationships within a whole class, a group of students, a relationship between a teacher, a student and their family, between colleagues, or between a faculty head and a member/s of the team.

2.1 Building Social Capital

Working restoratively is a way of *being and doing* that is both firm in terms of explicit standards of behaviour (boundaries and pressure) and fair in terms of supporting (nurturing) children, adolescents and adults to change their behaviour and develop pro-social thinking and skill-sets. In other words, if we are to live together in a learning community, our behaviours and relationships must reflect a deep knowledge and understanding of what it takes to be in cooperative relationships and to work within boundaries that provide safety for all. By doing so, a climate or environment for teaching and learning can be created, maintained and repaired when needed. That means our behaviours have to be regulated in a way that is authoritative rather than authoritarian, and where the relationship, so central to learning, as you will read shortly, is held at the centre of decision-making, but not at the expense of either standards or support. This is best illustrated in Figure 2.1, in an adaptation of Wachtel's (1999) representation of this.

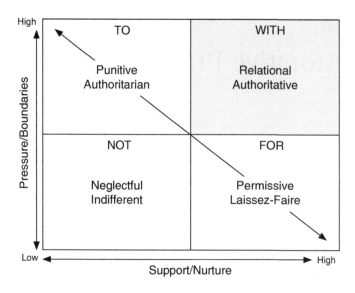

Figure 2.1 Social capital window (adapted from Wachtel 1999)

Each of the four quadrants represents a value placed on compliance (vertical axis) on the one hand, and the relationship (horizontal axis) on the other, which we describe in some detail.

- *Punitive/Authoritarian.* In the upper left-hand quadrant, this represents high pressure with low support. In this quadrant, the authoritarian approach demands compliance at all costs and punishes non-compliance. It's the adult's voice that matters, where children should be seen and not heard, and there is little engagement in problem-solving that is seen to be fair or just. The transaction can best be described by the words that punishment is done *to* or 'do what I tell you', rather than 'do what I do myself'.

- *Permissive/Laissez-Faire.* The quadrant diagonally opposite represents high support and low pressure. In this case, the child's needs and voice are dominant, with the needs of others taking a back seat and a state that, as Lahey (2013) indicates, represents 'high responsiveness and low demandingness' (p.13). It is often about a need for the adult to be liked, to be their friend, a fear of confronting what has happened, or in the case of parenting, over-protectiveness.

Coloroso (2003) explains how this is the position some modern ('jellyfish' or permissive) parents take, in an effort to not parent like their own parents. They have a tendency to sweep all obstacles from their children's lives, to give them everything they need and to do their problem-solving for them. You might know them as 'helicopter parents', always hovering around their child. This results in over-protection, excusing, rescuing or doing things *for* the child, rather than helping them to do it themselves. Over-protective parents raise helpless and powerless children who are 'destined for an anxious adulthood because they lack emotional resources which are required to cope with inevitable set backs and failure' (Lahey 2013, p.13). In a classroom, this can result in complete chaos and in the individual child can lead to lifelong poor problem-solving ability, boundary transgression and poor resilience. They do not learn to cope or to take responsibility for their actions.

- *Neglectful/Indifferent.* The lower left quadrant represents low pressure and low support. This is the space where the adult is not available for the child emotionally, psychologically or physically. There is little or no interaction and this approach is best described simply as *not* meeting the needs of others. Parents get to this place because they are struggling to cope in one way or another, due to unemployment, stress, drug and alcohol issues, ill health or mental health problems, to name a few. This can be transitory or long-term. Teachers get to this place because they are struggling professionally or personally and are struggling to meet the needs of their class.

- *Relational/Authoritative.* The final quadrant, where we believe the restorative philosophy of problem-solving works best, is distinguished by high pressure around expectations and standards in a climate of high support and nurture. This is the firm and fair aspect that we know works best for children and adults. We need to know the limits and we need to know that someone will be *with* us to help solve problems when we get ourselves into a mess. The emphasis is on repairing the harm we might have caused and helping us to take responsibility for our actions and to put in place strategies to avoid doing the same again. Together with the person or persons we have harmed, we will work out how to fix it. We will know, too, that we will end up feeling better about ourselves, and others, when we work things out this way. It is also the place where we might not know the answer to all problems, but together we will work it out in a fair and just way. It is a place of hope, collaboration, care and, above all, a position of high standards that we need to maintain, knowing that doing the right thing is not always easy.

Payne (2012) reminds us that if we are working successfully with young people to change their behaviour, three things need to be present: *support* (teaching explicitly what is needed), *high expectations* (pressure that comes from a relationship of mutual respect: 'I know you can do it, and you will') and *insistence* (the motivation and persistence that comes from a relationship of mutual respect). This looks an awful lot like working in the 'with' quadrant.

More broadly, RP is about effective behaviour and conflict management, predicated on the need for social and emotional wellbeing in schools. When we (the practitioner) are not working restoratively, it says more about what is happening for us (or our school) than it does about what happened and those involved. When we resort to punitive, permissive or neglectful ways of managing behaviour and conflict, there is something going on for us such as tiredness, stress or personal issues that lower our tolerance or coping abilities. Even when we mostly work restoratively, each of us has an Achilles heel or a vulnerability that can be triggered under duress. Awareness of our reaction and what triggers it is vital for recovering the situation and once again working in a more restorative or relational way. Being restorative is not something we turn on and off. Yet it does not preclude the need to set appropriate boundaries. We are aiming to be restorative at all times and, when we are not, we need to be aware of this and take responsibility for returning to the restorative frame. *It is a way of working that should inform everything we do. When we are not restorative, we have a case to answer.*

Case Study: Restorative Process Under Pressure

Sally was working with her class of senior students preparing them for a group assessment task. With a week to go, a member of one of the groups expressed tensions that had been building, despite indicators they were on target. Sally ran a restorative process, although the student that raised the alarm was not appeased by the group's explanation and apology to her. Sally asked her to reflect on what she needed and left the group to attend to other groups. The process had taken longer than Sally had hoped and she was now feeling anxious about the needs of the other groups. No sooner had she started to attend to another group when she was interrupted by a member of the first group to say that the student was refusing to work with them. Sally walked back into the room, raised her voice, pointed her finger, said it was unacceptable and demanded that the student see her after class to resolve the issue. Out of frustration, Sally slammed the door loudly on her way out of the room, making it clear she was angry.

In this case study, Sally had initially responded restoratively in a calm and caring way. Whilst doing so, she felt anxious about the needs of the other groups and the time she was investing in this one group. When it wasn't resolved and required more time, something in her was triggered and she responded in an authoritarian way. Whilst it would have been better to have caught the reaction before responding, she was aware of what had happened and willing to think about her reaction. Sally was able to calm down and deal with the student in a relational way. She apologised for raising her voice and explained the tension she felt in the student blocking any attempts to move forward. They were able to resolve the issue amicably. The next time Sally had the class, she apologised for what had happened, explained the anxiety that was present for her and how the issue had been resolved.

Working restoratively is about strengthening relationships and building community within the classroom and the wider school community. The effectiveness of RP is dependent on the quality of the existing relationships, how well we resolve issues and what else is happening in our school community. We become highly attuned to what is happening and what needs to happen to get us back on an even keel or to continue to work with the community to make a difference, as in the case of Sally. We no longer discount, tolerate, put up with or pretend that it is not going on and we avoid the blame game. We are alert to helping students, parents and staff to resolve their difficulties and we are aware that allowing something to remain unresolved is likely to lead to something else. We approach things from a perspective of needing to deal with them and we work with those involved to find the best solution to a problem or issues. We no longer deal in isolation or send students to isolation to work on their problems. We understand the different positions of those who have wronged and those that have been harmed and we work together to resolve that difference. Yet we acknowledge that we are human and will have our moments where it is difficult to maintain the restorative frame.

2.2 The Continuum of Practice

Wachtel and McCold (2001) describe 'the everyday use of a wide range of informal and formal restorative practices' (para. 13) which has now become widely accepted as something called a continuum of practice (see Figure 2.2).

The continuum describes a range of restorative practices that have evolved, and continue to evolve, with our greater understanding of the possibilities offered by the philosophy, skills and values embedded within RJ. Your school will eventually need to develop its own continuum of restorative practice and, rather than being too prescriptive here about what should appear in a school's protocols and procedures, we prefer to promote flexibility and innovation in order to meet the needs of a school community.

In Figure 2.2 we demonstrate how practice has been matched to the seriousness of an issue or incident. At one end of the continuum, the response is skilled, on the spot, relational for minor issues in classrooms and playgrounds. For slightly more serious incidents, the formality is increased and follow-up is generally required. At the serious 'pointy end', incidents that might trigger school removal or have caused serious harm tend to require very formal intervention and follow-up. Next we describe in a little more detail what we mean by the various processes we collectively refer to as restorative practice.

Minor incidents/issues

Affective statement
Relational conversation
Restorative 'chat'

Mini-conferences
Class meetings and problem-solving circles

Restorative/community conference
Restorative mediation healing circle
Class conferences (serious dysfunction)

Serious incidents/issues

Informal

Becoming more formal

Formal

Requires skill and little preparation
Informal follow-up

Requires reasonable skill and more preparation
Formal follow-up

Requires high-level skill and
comprehensive preparation
Formal follow-up

Figure 2.2 Continuum of practice (adapted from Wachtel and McCold 2001)

At the formal end of the continuum

The range of practices that may be considered at the formal end of the continuum may involve processes such as:

- restorative/community conference
- restorative mediation
- healing circle
- class conference.

The *restorative/community conference* is a facilitated meeting between the young person responsible for the harm (usually referred to as the wrongdoer), their family, the person (or people) harmed – either another student or students, and their family – together with key school managers and staff impacted by the incident. At this meeting, the young person is given an opportunity to explain what happened. The harm done to everyone – the primary victim, their family, friends, property (if necessary) and wrongdoer's family is explored so that that its depth and breadth is understood. The young person is given an opportunity to acknowledge this harm and to apologise. The group *together* decides what is needed to be done to repair the harm, and puts plans in place to prevent further harm and provide follow-up. The process is inclusive and where possible involves the key stakeholders in the process, with a primary aim to repair the harm that has been done.

Restorative mediation is the term applied to the process of bringing (usually) two parties together to negotiate a resolution to their differences/issues. This mediation process differs from typical mediation because both parties are invited to explore the harm that the conflict is causing each other and wider afield, and they are invited, as far as possible, to find ways to make things as right as possible between themselves. The plan addresses the future as well as the present problem, and is aimed at rebuilding trust between both parties.

The *healing circle*, with its roots in First Nation indigenous practice in North America, is a process that has been adapted for use in many settings – community, schools, prisons and workplaces. In schools it can be used to 'provide a safe, reflective place for staff, students and families and the community to talk about what happened, to share how they were affected…to express their needs, and to offer ideas about how to move forward in a positive way' (Riestenberg 2012, p.163).

Also located at the formal end of the continuum is the most formal of class meetings, the *class conference*, reserved for the serious cases of classes that for a variety of reasons have failed to settle and have developed such difficult dynamics that wellbeing, safety, and teaching and learning are at risk for both teacher and students.

The facilitator in each of these scenarios must be carefully trained and highly skilled as the stakes are high for all participants. Significant harm has been done and people will be feeling anxious about the process and concerned about outcomes. Preparation must be done carefully, along with follow-up of agreed plans and preventative actions.

In the middle of the continuum

At this point, the grip on formality has been loosened slightly. The meetings might be smaller or less formal (hence the term 'mini'). A typical meeting might involve a teacher, a parent/caregiver and a student facilitated by a middle manager who helps this group work through an issue that has caused harm, develop a plan and arrange for follow-up. It might involve a group of students who have fallen out and who have come for help, or whose conflict is causing harm in the classroom or playground.

There might be an issue that is beginning to bubble in a classroom and the teacher and class recognise that it is interfering with learning so together they decide to have a class meeting/circle that invites everyone, in a structured, safe way to talk through how the problem is affecting them, and how they might together resolve the issues. The class might be so skilled already that students can take turns to facilitate such a circle; or the teacher might elect to facilitate, or ask a member of the Senior Leadership Team (SLT) to do so.

At this point of the continuum, school staff, and in particular middle managers, are sufficiently skilled to facilitate these less formal but equally important meetings. Preparation of participants is a key feature of these semi-formal processes, as is appropriate follow-up.

At the informal end of the continuum

In a restorative school, we would expect to see all adults skilled and able to handle the minor issues that pop up in classrooms, corridors and in playgrounds – 'on the run'. These sorts of incidents rarely require a heavy-handed response, but do require a skill-set firmly embedded as habits in our behaviours, underpinned by values that place the relationship at the heart of problem-solving. The adult responses are respectful, curious (appreciative enquiry), calm, deliberate, firm and fair. While we have mentioned only three strategies as examples, staff with a relational attitude will have developed their own ways to do this work and should be encouraged to share their ideas with colleagues.

The *affective statement* is the simple 'I' statement: '*I'm feeling* (state the feeling)…*because* (name the behaviour/s)…*and what I'd like to see happen is*…(state the action)'.

For example: 'Class, I'm feeling really uncomfortable, because people are hurting one another and what I would like to see happen is that we each keep our hands to ourselves during the game.' It is the beginning of a non-threatening, non-blaming conversation that lets the young person or class know very clearly that their behaviour is causing harm. If these ideas have already been explored in classrooms, it is likely that any reasonable young person will be able to adjust their behaviour, especially if there are good relationships in the class. It will be harder if this is missing.

Should the statement not have the desired outcome, then the response is slightly more formal and may move to a *problem-solving circle* or *restorative chat*. 'OK, everyone stop doing what you are doing, we need to sit down and talk about what's happening and how the unsafe behaviours are affecting everyone. Remember, this is what we agreed to do when there's a problem.'

The *relational conversation*, an idea developed by Jude Moxon, a highly respected restorative practitioner in New Zealand, is a common-sense approach built around the notion that if one needs to correct a young person about a small issue (such as a uniform infringement) it might be best to connect with them first before having to disapprove of the behaviour. Jude Moxon uses four guiding principles in these relational conversations, outlined as: connectedness, caring, values rather than rules and building on strengths of the young person to solve the issue (Moxon 2013, personal communication). For example:

> Hi Joe, nice to see you. How are you going today? Could we have a chat about your uniform? (*connectedness*)

> I don't want you to be cold, but is there another way you could keep warm? How about wearing something underneath that doesn't show? (*caring*)

> Wearing the uniform is about belonging and you belong here, so it is important that you wear it in a way that shows that. (*values*)

> I know you are clever enough to keep the small things small. Have a great day. (*belief in strength to solve the issue*)

The restorative 'chat' is an informal, though slightly structured, dialogue with one or a number of students involved in low-level conflict, disruption or wrongdoing. It can be a one-on-one (teacher and student) or teacher resolving an issue between two or more students, dependent on who has been involved and what needs to happen. Built around simple questioning, the aim of the dialogue is to build awareness of the harm done, give the person harmed, if present, a voice in the problem-solving, and develop a plan to fix the issue. Follow-up is, again, critical. Questions to the wrongdoer include:

> Tell me what happened.

> What were you thinking at the time?

> What have you thought about since?

> Who has been affected? How?

> What needs to happen to repair the harm?

Questions to the person harmed include:

> What did you think when____happened?

> How have you been harmed/affected?

> What has been the hardest or most challenging part?

> What would you like to see happen?

The questions are open-ended, non-threatening and, as Hopkins (2004) states, are focused on the immediate past (what happened), the present (the impact) and the future (what needs to happen). They also target thinking, feelings and actions/behaviour with the intent to resolve issues, repair harm and to move on. Wherever possible, we want to ensure that all involved are included in the dialogue and, through this, the issue is resolved. Reliance on one-on-one chat alone is rarely effective. It may take many of these conversations – this is a process to teach young people *how to think* about their behaviour. At a neurological level, we now understand that we are creating new neural pathways in young brains, and there is no quick fix that does this!

2.3 A Whole School Approach

While educators in schools across the world have developed and are still developing a wide range of practices that fit on this formal–informal responsive continuum, we have long realised that:

> Effective behaviour management is the result of many interacting and complex factors, not the least of which are relevant, engaging curriculum and productive pedagogies. Restorative practice, with its emphasis on relationships, demands that schools attend to all aspects of the school culture and organisation and that they develop a range of relational practices that help prevent incidents of inappropriate behaviour from arising in the first place. (Blood and Thorsborne 2005, para. 3)

If we are to move beyond RP being seen as little more than another behaviour management strategy or response to significant issues of harm, then we must focus our attention on proactive strategies to resolve underlying issues and to prevent them from re-occurring.

Proactive responses are often informed by what is happening within the school environment. Many of the problems encountered in a typical school day are frequently misdiagnosed if not viewed through a relational lens and its exploration of factors contributing to relationship breakdown. For example: problems in playgrounds are often personalised and viewed as non-compliance on the part of an individual or groups of students. Restorative dialogue with the 'offending' parties often reveals factors that can be remedied without resorting to punishment (e.g. a lack of social skills, not knowing the game rules, boredom, poor allocation of play space or the lack of equipment). In Figure 2.3 we add this to the continuum of practice as we outline a layered whole school approach.

In Figure 2.3, there are three distinct layers of practice and each has a different intent, either to deal with conflict and disruption or to prevent it from occurring. The two top layers are our restorative, responsive continuum (repairing and reconnecting) and the bottom layer is about preventing issues from occurring and building healthy relationships (preventing and building). We describe this as the twofold ability to respond to what is happening and to consciously work to strengthen relationships and prevent issues from occurring. For successful implementation, it is critical that all three layers of practice are eventually in place. An important consideration is how much resourcing you put into each level and who is being targeted at each level (whole school community).

The preventative, proactive layer of the triangle is the business of all the adults of the school community – to deliver programmes and curriculum to all learners in order to develop their social and emotional competence, to develop their personal and interpersonal effectiveness, to contribute to a sense of belonging, safety and wellbeing in the school community so that learning can be maximised. In short, it is about developing a culture of care and respect. Morrison (2007) draws parallels to a health care model, where a universal or 'immunisation' programme might be employed as a preventative strategy (p.107), although this may also involve targeted programmes for students when the underlying cause of problems is discovered. For example, in the case of Lewisham Primary School referred to earlier, it was discovered that most of the children coming under notice were dealing with major grief and loss due to changing countries, family crisis or another important loss or upheaval in their lives. As a result, a specialised grief and loss programme was run to assist them to manage the underlying grief, with great success in terms of helping the students involved to cope. It was proactive, yet targeted.

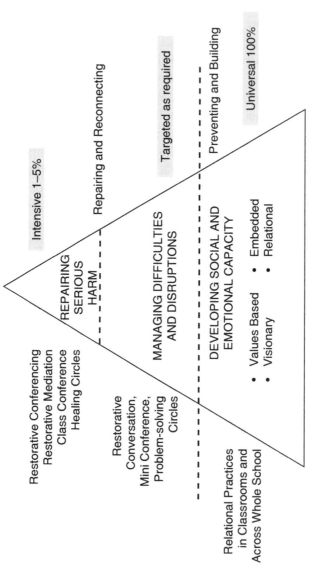

Figure 2.3 A whole school approach

At the middle level, it is critical that the whole school community (including casual teaching staff, administrative personnel and other support staff) is trained to manage the day-to-day difficulties. They need to be able to respond to the typical disruptions and difficulties that emerge when adults and children are required to work, learn and play in proximity with one another. It is important that staff have the capacity to notice and to respond effectively to what is happening in the school, or to get assistance if they feel unable to manage this themselves. At this level of practice, we would see and hear processes occurring in corridors, classrooms and in the playground. At an adult level, RP would be used to have those challenging conversations and to work through issues that arise in teams, staffrooms and faculties. RP is not something that is done to children, it is a way of working across the whole school community. This includes how adults deal with adults.

2.4 The Link between Pedagogy, Social and Emotional Literacy and RP

The ability of RP to make a difference is dependent on the quality of relationships within the school community and the overall health of a school. Effective behaviour management is virtually impossible without a healthy relationship between the student and the disciplinarian (Kohn 1996; Johns and Carr 2002). At the same time, any exploration of behaviour management will inevitably lead to discussions about curriculum and pedagogy, with the three intrinsically linked. Understanding the linkages between all three is a critical part of implementation of RP based on relational values. We will consider the necessary elements of social and emotional wellbeing, before examining the link between pedagogy and RP.

Social and emotional literacy

Marilyn Tew (2007) states that 'when people have a positive sense of themselves they are more open to new experiences, more flexible and willing to embrace change and therefore more able to learn' (p.9). We refer to this as social and emotional wellbeing, although there are a host of other such terms and ways to describe this, including emotional literacy, Social and Emotional Literacy (SEL) and Social and Emotional Aspects of Learning (SEAL). To be clear, we will define what we mean and outline the importance of building strong social and emotional wellbeing in your school community. Without this, nothing else is complete. We will focus on how connectedness and relational practices (including circles) can strengthen relationships and develop social and emotional literacy in classrooms, staffrooms and across the school community.

In order to develop healthy relationships we need to develop the social and emotional capacity within the classroom and staffroom.

Definition of social and emotional literacy

Elbertson, Brackett and Weissberg (2010) draw on the Collaborative for Academic, Social and Emotional Learning's [CASEL] working definition of Social and Emotional Learning (SEL) as: 'the acquisition of skills including self- and social awareness and regulation, responsible decision making and problem-solving, and relationship management' (p.1017). CASEL (2011) describes SEL as 'a process for helping children and even adults develop the fundamental skills for life effectiveness. SEL teaches the skills we all need to handle ourselves, our relationships, and our work, effectively and ethically' (para. 1). CASEL's (2011) core competencies for SEL are:

- *self-management* – managing own emotions and behaviours to achieve goals

- *self-awareness* – recognising own emotions, values, strengths and challenges

- *social awareness* – having understanding and empathy for others

- *relationship skills* – working together, managing conflict and forming positive relationships

- *responsible decision-making* – making good decisions and choices about personal and social behaviour.

These are the essential skills for life that, over time, ensure that children, young people and adults are more likely to be socially responsible, better parents, team players, employees and leaders.

As Elbertson *et al.* (2010) state, 'children who engage in positive social interactions with their teachers, peers, and families and who participate actively and cooperatively in the learning process are more successful in and out of school' (p.1018).

Early childhood expert, Dr Louise Porter, in an Australian Broadcasting Commission [ABC] (2002) interview for *Life Matters*, states that this process needs to start when children are three and four years old, so they start building a sense of:

- responsibility for self and others

- accountability in terms of the ability to distinguish right from wrong in the absence of an adult telling them

- ability to cooperate and work with others, even when they don't feel like it

- personal potency, so that they know they can make choices that are right for them and right for others, that they can take responsibility for themselves and for others, know right from wrong and that they can make a difference.

Tew (2007) cites five domains of emotional literacy and the constructs that help children and young people to do well at school:

1. *self-awareness* – optimism, imagination, integrity, confidence

2. *self-control* – managing emotions such as anger

3. *understanding others* – empathy, being helpful

4. *getting on with others* – working together, fitting in and communicating well

5. *motivation* – keeping going and staying on track.

Having a sense of self-awareness and self-control, combined with sense of 'other'-ness and knowing how to get along with them, motivates students to do well at school. The more students are skilled in each construct, the more likely they are to achieve success in school and beyond.

Steiner (1997; as cited in Tew 2007), indicates that to be emotionally literate we need to have the ability to:

1. understand emotions

2. listen and empathise with emotions

3. express emotions productively.

When we have this, we have personal power, are in command of our self, interact in positive and productive ways, and are more likely to be optimistic, resilient and to improve the relationships around us.

The link between restorative practice and SEL

Building SEL needs to be something that we are consciously working on, on a daily basis (the base of the triangle in Figure 2.3), on a weekly basis in terms of social emotional building programmes (circles and other pro-social skilling programmes and activities) and on a targeted basis (special SEL groups to deal with issues within the school, for groups and for individuals). This is dependent on understanding the issues within each community and the broader school population, whilst being responsive and creative to meeting these needs.

Tew (2007) offers guidance on how this needs to be developed, citing how teachers need to be the role models for how they expect children to interact and behave in school. From a restorative perspective, they need to be relational and to model how to deal with conflict and disruption in a relational way. They need to facilitate learning in relational ways to develop a healthy classroom environment that is conducive to learning. This requires teacher skills – to develop social and emotional literacy in the classroom, so that students are able to work cooperatively. As Lahey (2013) states, teaching SEL through activities and interactions within the classroom is among the most important things that a teacher can teach, the ones that will most assist students through their life's journey. Students and the whole class need to be able to discuss what is happening at the academic and at a social/emotional learning level and programmes and activities that develop their skills need to be built into the curriculum. This includes creating a range of opportunities for successes for students at an academic, social, emotional and personal level and the opportunity to learn from their mistakes.

These are the very skills young people need in order to solve problems in non-violent ways and to develop as responsible young citizens. What we have witnessed in schools implementing RP effectively in classrooms is not only 'standard' SEL competencies being implicitly and explicitly taught, but students being deliberately taught how the RP processes work and how to participate effectively. When there is an identified gap in student understanding, these schools are proactive in building the social and emotional literacy of those students, to be able to work with RP, rather than saying that 'our students don't have the language for this to work'. Many schools, wisely, have extended this 'this is how RP works, and this is how you participate properly' to the parent community in order to minimise the paradigm gap between parents and school.

The link between pedagogy and RP

Let's first consider the link between RP and the core business of schools – teaching and learning, otherwise referred to as pedagogy. Sahlberg (2012) indicates that consistent and good educational outcomes, the type that have led Finland to lead the world, require high quality professional leadership. Lingard *et al.* (2003) take the position that student learning, both academic and social, needs to be the core imperative of school leadership. That 'the task of school leadership, is above all, to lead learning by creating and sustaining the conditions that maximize both academic and social learning' (Lingard *et al.* 2003, p.2). It is the social learning and the environment that is conducive to learning that is often left on the sidelines whilst teachers meet the learning imperatives at an academic and curriculum level. MacNeill and Silcox (2003) discuss the importance of pedagogic leadership, citing how 'a principal must be leading an effective school, and a teacher must be effective in all aspects of the teaching act' (para. 8). Without this, it is difficult for teachers to teach and children to learn.

As MacNeill and Silcox (2003) indicate, school leaders need to lead schools that enable teachers to be effective in all aspects of their teaching. To do so, school leaders need to have a sound understanding of pedagogic practice, so that they are able to align staff with the vision and direction of the school and to support them in their practice. The Senior Leadership Team (SLT) also needs to make the link between RP and pedagogy crystal clear, to help teachers make sense of why they are doing this, and how it helps them to teach and children to learn. This is particularly so when a teacher's initial response to proposals for introducing RP into the classroom is: 'I haven't got time to do this – I have to get through the curriculum.'

In an extensive research study, Lingard *et al.* (2003) found that academic outcomes are enhanced when schools have a strong emphasis and focus on the quality of relationships as part of that learning environment. This is something that often gets lost in the pressures of standardised testing in place in many education systems. Lingard *et al.* (2003) also found that schools with a strong relational focus were found to have enhanced learning outcomes. This aligns with the world-class Finnish education system, which has built a leading education system on most measures. It is a system that does not employ any standardised testing, instead focusing on access and equality in education delivered by highly qualified and reflective practitioners, employed in good schools led by qualified educational leaders (Sahlberg 2012).

Whilst there are many pedagogical models, we will draw on just one as a way of making the pedagogical links between RP and the academic aspect of learning. Gore, Griffiths and Ladwig (2004) cite the four dimensions of the productive pedagogy framework as: intellectual quality, relevance, social support and recognition of difference (see Figure 2.4), indicating that productive pedagogy 'explicitly attends to both intellectual and social justice outcomes' (pp.376–377). RP clearly assists in achieving social justice outcomes through the creation of explicit and high expectations and positive relationships between students and between teachers and students, and helps to develop high quality learning environments. Together with high expectations, RP offers high support to develop self-regulating students and classrooms.

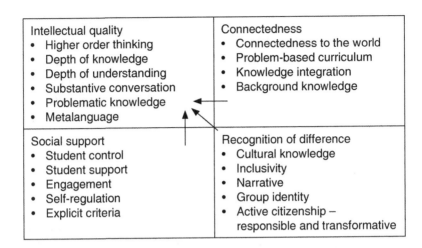

Intellectual quality	Connectedness
• Higher order thinking • Depth of knowledge • Depth of understanding • Substantive conversation • Problematic knowledge • Metalanguage	• Connectedness to the world • Problem-based curriculum • Knowledge integration • Background knowledge
Social support	Recognition of difference
• Student control • Student support • Engagement • Self-regulation • Explicit criteria	• Cultural knowledge • Inclusivity • Narrative • Group identity • Active citizenship – responsible and transformative

Figure 2.4 Productive pedagogy (adapted from Lingard *et al.* 2003)

In Figure 2.4, we have adapted Lingard *et al.*'s (2003) four dimensions of pedagogy to indicate how RP helps to develop the intellectual quality in classrooms, by assisting in building connectedness in the classroom, social support and recognition of difference. Working restoratively and relationally helps to build classrooms where all students are recognised and valued, where there is high support and high expectations, where these are clear and students learn to self-regulate and assist in regulating the behaviour of their peers. Helping students to resolve their difficulties and skilling them in SEL, helps to build connectedness, inclusivity, group identity and responsible and active citizenship.

Attending to what is going on beneath the presenting behaviour
So far we have discussed the layers of practice required for whole school change and the continuum of practices. Whilst we will look at the preventative proactive strategies of building social emotional literacy next, a conversation which is often missed is the one about attending to what is going on beneath presenting behaviour. As Bonnor and Caro (2012) state, 'student welfare stands alongside teaching and learning at the heart of everything a good school does…students cannot learn properly if they are distracted by issues at home, or by anxiety or depression' (p.116). Facilitating

connectedness among peers in an environment that is conducive to the development of healthy standards of behaviour is a critical risk reduction strategy (Kirby 2001; as cited in Whitlock 2003, para. 1). As we have seen time and time again, schools that develop a healthy school environment not only have enhanced learning outcomes and better behaved young people, but young people and teenagers who come from troubled backgrounds are more likely to see school as a safe haven, one where they can put their troubles behind them for the time they are in school.

RP necessarily starts with the presenting issue and the need to address what happened in that moment or the lead-up to it. To rescue or excuse the behaviour would be akin to what happens in the court system, where once an offender is found guilty, the defence seek to mitigate the severity of the punishment with the circumstance that may have informed the act itself (he was drunk and unaware of what he was doing, had a bad upbringing, just broke up with his girlfriend). For victims of serious crime, these mitigations can be devastating to hear, especially as the court process leaves little room for victims or their families to have a say. This is no more evident than in the various stories we hear from families who have sat in court listening as the process wears on and the voices of their loved ones appear to be forgotten or ignored (Virk 2008; Hutchison 2006; Garner 2004). Necessarily the case is focused on proving the case against the offender, whilst the person or people harmed become secondary, often spoken of in depersonalised ways such as 'the deceased' or 'the victim'. For victims, there seems to be no connection between the impact of the crime on them and what might have informed the behaviour that so affected them. The two do not equate, especially when the system keeps both victims and offenders apart with no chance for dialogue. Similarly in schools it is too often the case that the focus is on student behaviour, whilst challenging adult relationships are ignored or tolerated.

Staff relationships

We cannot write about RP with students and not raise the issue about staff relationships and how these are both created by the culture and contribute to the culture. Simpson (2004) refers to cultural cues, for example, that new staff are confronted with when they settle in to a new school. We have adapted some of the cues from his list for the school setting and added a number of others for consideration. They include:

- how management speak to staff

- how staff speak about the management in their absence

- how management and staff speak about students and parents

- what are the patterns of communication in staff meetings and what is said immediately after a meeting

- how criticism and disagreement are handled

- how the school invites, promotes and supports initiatives and individual vision, and

- how the school responds to identified need amongst students or staff.

What are the cultural cues in your school? How is business done? How do people communicate with one another?

Case Study: A Permissive School

Peta once walked into a primary school to run some professional development only to be told by an unfriendly office staff member to make her way to the staff room. Like many schools, the school was a rabbit warren of corridors, making it very difficult to find the correct room. Fearing she was lost, she asked a student if she was going in the right direction, to which the student swore at her and offered no help. At first willing to dismiss this as a case of a student having a bad day, then the same request was met with the same level of abuse from another student. Throughout the day (after finding the staffroom and relevant staff member), it became really clear that the culture of this school was for students to treat staff members with disrespect and for that to be tolerated by staff. When later asked what was happening in the school, the staff unanimously replied, 'That's the way they behave at home, so what do you expect?' Peta responded: 'A whole lot more!'

It was an indication that staff had become resigned to a culture of disrespect, and if the behaviour of the front office staff was anything to go by, had absorbed the same values and behaviour in order to fit in. If they believed change was even possible and they wanted things to be different, then looking deeply into values and their messages was a matter of some urgency.

Corporate Culture, a consultancy and pioneer of culture work in Australia, agrees, defining culture as:

> Culture is the result of messages that are received about what is really valued. People align their behaviour to these messages in order to fit in. Changing culture requires a systematic and planned change to these messages, whose sources are behaviour, symbols and systems. (Taylor 2004, p.3)

Taylor (2004) encourages us to understand that culture management (and therefore culture change) is about message management. Staff are constantly watching the Executive staff and those considered part of the leadership group for the behavioural cues they are sending. Their actions send messages to people about what is expected around the school, as are the messages from symbols: actions, decisions and situations visible to a large number of people from which they make meaning. Even small events can send big messages (e.g. how a senior manager might respond to a student sent to them by a classroom teacher for 'punishment' or the inappropriate communication around a staff issue). Highly visible symbols such as school priorities, school uniforms, where resources are allocated, and facilities tell us 'what is important around here', and conversely what is ignored.

Lee (2004), an Australian authority on leadership development and organisational change, agrees with Taylor's (2004) assertion that culture change is more effective when transformational in nature and begins with the organisation's leadership, stating that it must be 'driven by passionate and persistent leadership at the top. Therefore, transformational change begins with transforming the mind-sets of managers' (Lee 2004, p.39).

He does, however, warn us that organisations with a traditional culture no longer produce anywhere close to the results required or what is possible. It is also clear that such cultures are extremely resilient and, in fact, highly resistant to change. Those of us who have worked in schools with entrenched cultures can only agree that sometimes in such places this culture is hard to shift.

Our final comment about staff relationships at this point is more of a question for you. To what extent is the quality of professional, collegial relationships an important issue in your staffroom, team or faculty? How are issues handled? How transparent are decisions affecting staff? How engaged are the adults with each other?

Thorsborne (2011) writes:

> ...schools are also workplaces for adults. What works best between adults and students, also works for adults in their relationships with each other. If schools intend to implement restorative policy and protocols, they must pay close attention to the quality of staff relationships. If these are not positive, if there is little trust between management and staff, if there is a history of unresolved conflict, poor structures and processes, then staff will smell a rat and say: 'Why should we change our approaches with kids when our relationships with each other and our own well-being don't seem to matter?'

> To change the behaviour of the students in our classrooms and playgrounds, we must change our own behaviours. Adults first. But for the change process to be sustained, we must look to our own relationships with our colleagues. These should be a source of deep and mutual satisfaction. This does not happen by accident. Our relationships must be built and nurtured, and repaired when disconnections occur. We have to walk our talk with each other. (p.217)

Bringing it all together

When we bring this back to what is required for a whole school approach, we are suggesting that you cannot have RP *without* SEL and connectedness. The combination of both ends of the continuum (responsive and preventative) has a powerful potentiating effect. Couple this with sound pedagogical leadership to enable teachers to teach well, and leaders are able to create an environment that is conducive to both learning and healthy relationships. Underpinning this is a way of working with others in the school community that holds people to account (high demandingness) and supports them to teach and learn (high supportiveness) (Locke, Campbell and Kavanagh 2012). This demands a way of being, a way of responding to what is happening in a relational way that will assist schools to create an environment that develops healthy norms of behaviour.

Rozen (as cited in Arbinger Institute 2006) describes this way of being as the heart way (see Figure 2.5). Yusuf al-Falah, an Arab, and Avi Rozen, a Jew, discuss how they each lost their fathers at the hands of the others' ethnic cousins, yet went on to become great friends by the approach they took to conflict (in their case, war). In essence what al-Falah and Rozen are saying is that approaches to problem-solving (that is, our problem-solving *behaviours*) will come from a 'heart' that is either peaceful or at war. If we come from a place of war in our heart, then we dehumanise the other person or objectify them in ways that result in further harm. We see the young person as the problem or evil child. We then respond in punitive and punishing (heart of war) ways that do not deal with the underlying causal factors of the behaviour. If we take a peaceful approach (heart of peace), then we see people as people, not much different from ourselves with the same needs, cares, wants and fears. We will also seek to understand what is going on, how that child is struggling, and consider what we need to do to call them to account, whilst at the same time supporting them to change their behaviour.

RP is a way of being that requires leaders, schools and students to approach what is happening in the school community with peaceful hearts, rather than with hearts at war, where the head has already made up its mind to write off this parent, or teacher or child. No good can come of this approach. In fact for many students who are in a place of misbehaving, through little fault of their own, they go on to do immense harm to themselves and others, in part because of the heart of war they are met with over and over in their lives. With this view, the implementation of RP requires a substantial shift in thinking, or as we say – *a shift in the hearts and minds* of schools and the people that govern them, lead them and practise within them.

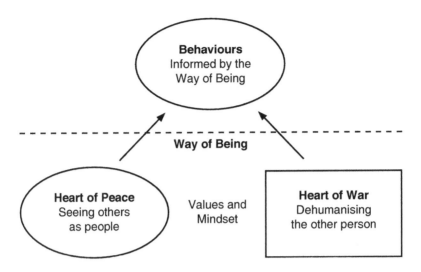

Figure 2.5 Way of Being diagram (adapted from Rozen, n.d.; as cited in The Arbinger Institute 2006)

Chapter 3

The Restorative School
Begin with the End in Mind

In this chapter we consider the nature of culture change and how the implementation of RP, as we have discussed, requires a shift in hearts and minds, or a paradigm shift in the ways schools work. Without this, RP will be less than effective, unless the school environment is already conducive to the development of healthy relationships. We begin with an overview of culture change and conclude with what a restorative school looks like, feels like and sounds like.

3.1 Cultural Change: Changing a Paradigm

Culture has been defined in many ways, but perhaps the simplest definition we have found is that it is *the way we do things around here* (Ouchi and Johnson 1978; Simpson 2004). Grange (2013) states that 'culture is a complex, multi-faceted, multi-layered phenomenon that is social, learned and transmitted between people. It is about behaviours, beliefs, symbols, norms and expectations. It grows over time and can be directed and shaped with strong leadership and sound methodologies' (p.3). Kotter (2012a) affirms this, stating that 'culture changes only after you have successfully altered people's actions' (p.164). Change on the other hand is variously designed as 'to transform, to make different in form, and to replace or substitute' (National Academy of Academic Leadership, n.d.).

RP has been variously described as 'the glue that holds everything together', a guiding set of principles or a framework for understanding effective school practice. This can require a significant shift in thinking on the part of educators and administrators who often have alternative views about their relationship to students in the classroom and about their behaviour. In Section 2 of this book we discuss how the implementation of restorative practice may involve either first or second order change. First order change involves the integration of restorative practice into what already exists, whilst second order change is about whole school transformation. The reality is that few schools are aware of this distinction, with the vast majority seeing RP as just another behaviour management strategy or 'tool' in the kitbag. This book does not support such a piecemeal approach; rather, it provides a guide for how RP can be successfully integrated into a school and how this work can help change the culture of a whole school community.

It is the challenging of mindsets where true culture change begins. Mezirow (2000) refers to this as the need to transform one's world view, where a critical part of any change process is the need for individuals to change their frame of reference by reflecting on and challenging their beliefs and assumptions. Far from wanting to overwhelm readers at this point in the book with the enormity of the task of setting about changing culture in a very traditional environment, we offer first some advice from prevailing management theory about culture change so that well-meaning effort, energy and enthusiasm are not wasted. Further reference to culture change is made in Sections 2 and 3 of this book.

3.2 The Restorative School

To this end, we ask you to think about what your school might look like if it had embraced the restorative philosophy, had successfully implemented a carefully planned strategy and was perhaps already in the maintenance phase, maybe three or five years on. But even if you have reached what you think is a good place, like any change we want to make permanent, it takes constant attention to maintain an organisation in such a pattern. So let's begin with the end in mind before we look at how to get there and what might get in the way of this.

Looks like, feels like, sounds like

If you walked into a restorative school and stayed long enough to see how things are done, what would you expect to see, hear and feel? What would be striking about this environment and the way people interacted?

The following list has been generated from conversations with schools and educational institutions in varying countries and settings; all schools that are on the restorative journey, in various states of implementation. Some schools have been on the path for many years, others are relative newcomers. We hope in time that this list may become more comprehensive as we learn more about successful implementation and the management of whole school change around school improvement. Use the following as a checklist to assess how far along the journey your school might be.

Values, attitudes and climate

- The attitude to learning and behaviour from both teachers and learners is unfailingly positive.

- Difficult moments are regarded as educational opportunities – indeed, as teachable moments.

- The school values are clearly defined for adults, students and parents in terms of expected behaviours and these behaviours are explicit, taught, known and modelled by all adults.

- Offending behaviour is viewed as a breach of relationships, against school community values.

- There is an inclusive approach to teaching and behaviour with the system aiming to keep students *at* school. There is an attitude of persistence among staff, parents and students that means that the school is unwilling to give up on difficult students or to want to get rid of them at the earliest opportunity. Young people are not demonised. The school sees its role as a partner in child-rearing with families – not always an equal partnership, but the school is prepared to step up nevertheless.

- The school is the hub of its local community both physically and metaphorically. Strong, positive, collaborative relationships are evident between the school, local police, local authorities/ councils, local agencies, local businesses and community groups. There is a whole-community approach to tackling the issues for young people and their families. This is seen as a shared responsibility and a challenge that the school embraces, rather than shies away from.

- There is a recognition, and commitment to the notion, that positive, robust relationships lie at the heart of learning and pedagogical practice, of wellbeing and a sense of belonging and connectedness; and all decisions, structures, policies and procedures reflect this understanding.

- There is an understanding of the need to restore relationships in the aftermath of conflict and wrongdoing or major incidents within the school. This is reflected in practice with the focus on problem-solving around the damage that needs to be fixed rather than the rule breach that needs to be punished.

- There is a comfortable marriage between the values of the school and the values of a restorative approach to problem-solving. Leadership is values-based and transformational, and leaders walk the talk, and model the required change.

- The school regards itself as a learning organisation, committed to continual improvement. Data is used effectively to inform discussion, debate and problem-solving. Data is used to address gaps, and reality is regularly interrogated.

- Visitors to the school are treated with respect, approached with a friendly greeting from students and adults, and are made to feel welcome. There is a high level of trust evident across and between members of the school and wider community.

- The school *feels* friendly, peaceful and polite. The school has a reputation for a focus on the positives, for its use of fair process, for academic excellence, for making a difference in the community. Enrolments might be increasing, rather than diminishing, and car park and supermarket conversations amongst parents about the school are positive.

- Everyone understands that the school community is never static, that the school membership is constantly altering and that what has worked for one cohort of students may not work for the next. The school is proactive, future-focused, and welcomes change.

- There is clear and effective dialogue from the top down, bottom up and between staff, students, parents and anyone engaged with the school community.

LINKS WITH CURRICULUM AND TEACHING AND LEARNING

- The restorative philosophy is embedded in and integrated into quality teaching and learning with clear linkages between key initiatives, system imperatives, pedagogy and key competencies so it is not seen as an add-on or stand-alone initiative. The approach is seen as the 'glue' that enhances the core business of teaching and learning within the school community – a framework for best practice.

- As part of relationship skill development, teachers are skilled in basic effective, innovative classroom management and pedagogy.

- Attention is paid to the quality of the relationships between learners as well as between teacher and learner, in recognition of the need for an optimal environment for learning – a sense of safety and belonging.

- The school has a stimulating emotional environment where interest and enjoyment are maximised for learners and teachers alike. Impediments to this are appropriately addressed.

- The behaviour of learners is not seen as a separate issue to be managed outside the curriculum. Regular class meetings are held to develop social and emotional competencies, self-regulation and whole-class responsibility for the climate in the classroom. Students are explicitly taught the skills required to participate in restorative processes.

- There is effective communication and collaboration between pastoral care and curriculum roles (e.g. classroom teachers, deans, heads of house, syndicate leaders and heads of faculty/department) when behaviour issues arise in classrooms.

- Induction for new staff and learners is taken seriously and adequately resourced. There is a prominent focus on the restorative approach to problem-solving.

- Transitions for learners are well managed: between schools, within school from one year level to the next, or between sub-schools and subject changes so that a strong sense of connectedness and/or closure is an outcome.

- A case management approach is taken to address issues around particular learners, with preparedness to work on underlying issues as well as the symptomatic behaviours. The school is well connected to providers that can assist with student and family issues.

- Restorative practice/relationship competence is built into the school's appraisal, selection and recruitment processes.

RESTORATIVE PRACTICE

- There is a well-developed continuum of practice that can be adapted readily to situations from serious to minor. The continuum is understood by learners, teachers, school administrators and parents and is outlined in staff and student handbooks.

- There is a whole school approach to the restorative philosophy and a consistency of practice and philosophy across the whole school (teachers, support staff and school administration) so that everyone understands why the restorative approach is used and can trust the systems in place.

- The school addresses the harm from inappropriate behaviour and incidents in a way that:

  - deals with conflict and disruption in a timely manner

  - repairs harm in the aftermath of wrongdoing

  - addresses issues with all involved

- works with those involved to find the best solution for what has happened
- embraces a diversity of solutions by understanding that there may be many ways to solve a problem
- focuses on what needs to happen to repair harm
- looks at what needs to happen to prevent further harm.

• The overall focus is on developing positive relationships between students, teachers, parents and the wider community. This also means that energy is spent on developing social and emotional competence and positive behaviours so that young people have the capacity to engage effectively in restorative problem-solving.

• Both practice and practitioners are reflective and the school is intent on developing best practice. With a combination of positive pressure and support, the adults are held accountable for their practice as professionals.

• Leaders have had intensive training in the range of restorative practices – they understand the philosophy and processes from the inside out. Restorative process becomes the default approach to problem-solving and leaders and middle managers lead by example with this approach.

• Learners are taught about the approaches to problem-solving so that they can actively and effectively participate. Eventually there is evidence that they are using these approaches to solve their own problems at school and at home; parents request restorative processes when there is a problem.

• Practice is adapted for particular settings within the school community (early years, primary, middle years, secondary and beyond, special needs, alternate settings).

• Staff conflict is acknowledged and acted on with a restorative approach, with all adults having a clear understanding of the need to model what we want from young people. We must be prepared to use the same approach for the issues that arise for us. If the school does not have enough skill to manage such issues, then it must be prepared to access external help.

- There is an alignment of philosophy, policy and practice. Any behaviour management policy is framed in positive terms such as 'Relationship' policy, 'Care and Responsibility' policy or 'Respect' policy.

- Dialogue about learners, their families or staff issues shifts from blame to flexible problem-solving evidenced in practice, language and actions. Problems are seen as opportunities to refine existing practice.

- *Everyone's* voice is important, not just the voice of adults within the school community. There is more *listening*, and less *telling*.

- The school is very clear about what *is* negotiable and what *isn't* in terms of rules, limits and boundaries in classrooms and playgrounds – the learner experiences the school and the adults as firm, fair and flexible and the rules make sense to children and adults alike. Boundaries are generated and abandoned as needed (Richmond 2009).

- Roles have been re-negotiated around *who is responsible* for managing behaviour and learning issues to increase the involvement and responsibility of classroom teachers. The person who owns the relationship with the troublesome student is central to the problem-solving and healing the relationship is a strong focus. Middle managers are expected to take a restorative approach to problem-solving and this is built into their role statements.

- The issue of zero tolerance is viewed as 'we don't accept that behaviour in our school', rather than one of excluding students based on their behaviour. Schools show this by taking the issue seriously and defaulting to a restorative approach where possible (e.g. using RP for drug issues, rather than immediate no-negotiation exclusion).

- Professional development for adults takes a high priority and is resourced to reflect this; not only around responding to new curriculum and system imperatives, but keeping 'relationships' front and centre, and there is balance between these two often-competing pressures.

- Collegial, professional relationships among staff have been developed and the dialogue reflects 'the problem is the problem' rather than regarding difficult behaviours with deficit thinking and pathologising of young people and their families. Language used is solution-focused and avoids blame.

- Older students are skilled up to help sort lower-level/minor issues with younger students, supported by the adults in the school ready to step in if a matter requires their attention. Students do not do the work of the adults.

- There is adequate resourcing attached to implementation and maintenance. Key staff are allocated time for more complex or serious cases; there might be a coordinator appointed to oversee implementation.

- There is a strategic plan within the school's annual plan that addresses RP implementation and maintenance and has its own defined budget.

- Attention is paid to follow-up, data collection and analysis. There is a data-driven approach to problem-solving that is aimed at school improvement and addressing gaps in learning, behaviour and practice.

- In the case of performance issues, a restorative approach is the first option, before more serious sanctions become necessary. Problems are not left to fester and/or escalate.

If the above list looks like a huge job, it absolutely is! There are no quick fixes for changing people's perceptions, beliefs and paradigms. Shifting thinking and behaviours of a whole school community takes time. That is why the rest of this book is devoted to the need for understanding, planning and strategically managing the change process if you are to successfully integrate and implement restorative practice in your school.

We have written this book so that change agents, consultants, school administrators, trainers and implementation teams understand how to better engage the people involved in and affected by the change process so that it is more likely that unnecessary resistance won't make this harder than needed. Indeed, resistance can be tackled in a way that actually strengthens relationships across the school community.

The following sections in this book will provide you with a systematic and strategic approach to implementation, because nothing succeeds better than a decent plan. But it is the *execution* of the plan that will bring people towards a vision of new possibilities; and the recognition that it is a winning of hearts as well as minds that is every bit as important as the plan itself. To that end, we have written our next chapter on managing the change process so we understand what is involved. We hope staff will not experience the implementation of restorative practice as an imposition, but rather as a willing investment. We hope they see the worth of the effort because it will improve educational outcomes for learners by maximising interest and enjoyment, and minimising the more toxic emotions that impede learning and job satisfaction.

Managing the Change Process

Chapter 4

Understanding the Change Process

The starting place for understanding change is to know what it is that you are trying to achieve. The success and sustainability of restorative practice requires an intrinsic understanding that this is:

> not an add-on programme for the purposes of behaviour management, nor does it provide just another tool in the toolbox for staff to use to deal with student behaviour. In contrast, restorative school discipline represents a school culture that permeates all aspects of school organization and relationships within the school as well as relationships between the school and its community. (Meyer and Evans 2012, p.5)

Change is a complex process and one that will probably fail if you do not capture the hearts and minds of your people and do not approach the implementation in a systematic way. In Section 3 of this book, we discuss how to manage the change process in a careful strategic way. In this section we look at the nature of change, and in particular how to bring people on board in the process, by considering Rogers' (2003) Diffusion Model of Change that we introduced in our 2005 paper on this topic (Blood and Thorsborne 2005). We also examine the emotional dynamics of change – that is, how it impacts on people, and how to work with this. Change is unsettling at the best of times, let alone when it is not managed well. Far better to be warned before you start than wonder what happened to a worthy change initiative. Whilst we will talk about some of the specifics in terms of the implementation of restorative practice in an educational context, this applies to any change, in any setting. Basically, you are dealing with human beings and the range of human emotions triggered by change. Unless you understand how people react to change, what their concerns are, what they need and how you can address this, you will be left wondering what happened.

We also look specifically at why change fails and how to overcome resistance by addressing the various concerns and needs that people have. After examining the pitfalls of change, we also ask you to be clear about what type of change you are looking for and whether first order or second order change is required. Understanding this will help you to determine your priorities in this area. We then look at the elements of effective change initiatives, bringing in a range of perspectives from some well-known authors in the field of leadership and change management. Finally, we examine the role of leadership and attention to the ongoing issues of leadership and change management throughout the implementation process. Paying relentless attention to these will have its payoffs.

> If you have identified yourself as having previously led a change initiative that failed, you can always start again in terms of putting effective change management in place. But to do so, you might have to use your restorative skills in a meeting of key staff to take responsibility for what has happened to date. Here is an example of what you might say:
>
> As you know, we introduced restorative practice some time back into our school. We have implemented RP with varying degrees of success to date, and I am aware that many of you have been questioning the validity of this process. Part of the issue, now that we think it through, is that we told you it was going to happen, without awareness of what it would take to develop practice to a place of making a real difference.
>
> So what we would like to do is start now by asking you what *is* working and what's *not* working and what resources and support you need to put this into practice.

Remember, a lot of this is trial and error and we have only been able to develop our thinking through riding these ups and downs with schools in the early days of practice and implementation. When we both started this work, in the 1990s, restorative practice was seen as just another behaviour management tool in an educator's toolbox, as the quote at the start of this section by Meyer and Evans (2012) highlights. Whilst a very handy tool, it was overlaid on top of existing school disciplinary practices that were often punitive and reactive in nature.

It was through this early experience that the range of practices was developed and embedded to the point where it became 'what we do routinely around here', rather than something we only do occasionally when there is a problem. Our focus gradually broadened to thinking about how to prevent incidents from occurring in the first place, through relational practices and catching small issues early before they escalated. The continuum of practices led to a range of possibilities and existing practices and structures were sufficiently challenged to force change.

Through working with many schools in many countries and our own extensive research into change management and effective leadership, we have learnt what gets in the way of the successful change and how to better manage the change process. In this section of the book, we consider how to manage this change process in order to develop an environment that is conducive to change.

4.1 Rogers' Diffusion Model of Innovation

In our 2006 paper, *Overcoming Resistance to Whole-School Uptake of Restorative Practices*, we considered the best way to understand and explain the process of change and to assist schools to approach this. We believe that Rogers' (2003) Diffusion Model of Innovation has much to offer in this regard, especially in understanding how people progress through any change initiative. We start here by building an understanding of his model of innovation, considering what people need and the groups you will need to persuade and influence. We will then explore the notion that change is an emotional process and what people need at an emotional level to cope with a change they might not have asked for or agree with, at least in the first instance. In other words, what do we need to do to capture hearts and minds?

Rogers (2003) explains that innovation creates uncertainty, and because it is such an uncomfortable state, individuals seek information about the new idea and its capacity to solve problems from their peers. 'The diffusion of innovations is essentially a social process in which subjectively perceived information about a new idea is communicated from person to person' (Rogers 2003, p.xx). How this information is communicated is what we deal with in Section 3 of our book, particularly in Step 4 Communicating the Vision – Capturing Hearts and Minds. Communication between people is what we are concerned with here, along with building awareness of what needs to be addressed to ensure that the implementation of restorative practice is likely to succeed.

Rogers (2003) suggests that the main elements of the diffusion of new ideas such as the implementation of restorative practice are that the *innovation* (restorative practice) must be *communicated* through certain channels, *over time, among the members* of the school community. Whilst we refer to the implementation of restorative practice, this might apply to any change initiative. Rogers (2003) states that:

1. An innovation is any idea, practice or object that is perceived as new by those that are considering its adoption, such as the implementation of whole school change.

2. The innovation is communicated through various channels to those that are required to adopt, or may be considering adopting, the idea, practice or object (introduction, seminar, peers, training, etc.).

3. Innovation takes time to implement and its rate of adoption is dependent on a range of factors. This might also be referred to as the decision-making process where those considering adoption either accept the idea or reject it. Clarke (1999) outlines five stages of the decision-making process first articulated by Rogers (2003) as:

   (a) *knowledge* (exposure to its existence, and understanding of its functions)

   (b) *persuasion* (the forming of a favourable attitude to it)

   (c) *decision* (commitment to its adoption)

   (d) *implementation* (putting it to use), and

(e) *confirmation* (reinforcement based on positive outcomes from it).

4. Each social system has its own set of norms and established patterns of behaviour among its members. In this instance, every school has its own culture and sub-cultures within it. When educators make the claim that 'our school is unique', at a cultural level they are right. The implementation of restorative practice will challenge these norms and established behaviours, increasing the likelihood of resistance to change when the status quo is threatened. Whilst some will be enthusiastic for change, having already expressed or held concerns about the established way of doing things, some will complain and be unwilling to change; others yet will adopt a wait-and-see approach as many change processes have gone before them, whilst others will steadfastly block any change initiative.

Rogers (2003) outlines how to work with these different groups, by first placing them into different categories according to the rate they adopt change. People take up change at differing rates and that makes a difference in the way we work with them. Their distribution under a bell curve can be seen in Figure 4.1, where he defines five categories of people that he refers to as the Innovators, Early Adopters, Early Majority, Late Majority and Laggards.

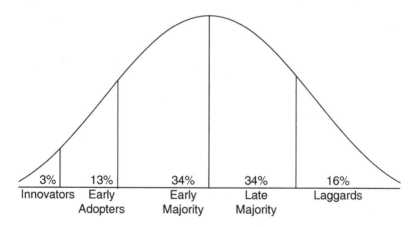

Figure 4.1 Rogers' (2003) Diffusion Model of Innovation

Whilst the characteristics of each group that we will describe are helpful in understanding some of the barriers to implementation, it is not intended that you label people in the process. We firmly believe that the more aware we are of what people need to navigate change, the more effective planning for the change process will be. You could consider this model a bit of a continuum, as people will change groups dependent on the change initiative they are asked to adopt. People may be in different groups at different times, such as the teacher who is an innovator in a subject area and part of the Late Majority when it comes to the adoption of restorative practice. Someone else may be completely resistant to a new idea if past ideas have failed or relationships in the school community have become unsafe for them. Nothing is fixed about this – especially when it comes to managing people's attitude to changes we ask of them.

We will now describe the characteristics of each group and later explore ways of managing each group throughout the implementation process.

Innovators

Innovators are the type of people who are on the lookout for new and promising ideas in their field of interest. They are visionary people and are able to grasp new concepts and apply them to their own unique setting. They have a huge capacity for networking, particularly outside their own organisation. Innovators are risk-takers who can cope with the uncertainty of change – in fact they embrace change processes with a vigour that can leave others reeling in their wake. The sad reality is that this group may not hold a large sphere of influence among their peers or subordinates. *But they have an important role in seeking new initiatives and bringing them into the system.*

Innovators have a tendency to fall into two groups: those that embrace all the latest new ideas and are almost addicted to the change process or to new ideas; and those who are constantly looking for what can make a difference in their field. The first group will often be spoken about in quite disparaging ways, whilst the latter will be admired by some for their passion and will frighten the living daylights out of others. Comments of 'here we go again', 'what now' and 'what is she or he up to this time' often follow this group.

For this reason, innovators cannot successfully embed innovation alone. Not only do they represent only three per cent of an organisation (Rogers 2003), they often lack credibility within their own system. Their talents are best used to encourage and support Early Adopters to pick up an idea and run with it, provided they are given the opportunity to experiment to see if the idea has merit and will work.

Innovators can make a difference and lead substantial change initiatives. However, they need to know how much is enough. Given a school in crisis or in need of change, an Innovator will bring fresh and creative ideas into the school environment and provided they encourage buy-in, they can turn a school environment around quite quickly, or at least get the change process started. The rate of adoption of change is significant in the early days as staff previously starved of good ideas and participation relish the opportunity to be involved, with those that are sceptical more likely to take the opportunity to change schools on the arrival of the Innovator. Once the initial crisis is over, however, Innovators can struggle to allow an innovation to settle before they embark on the next lot of change, without giving staff the ability to stop and catch up on an initiative. Innovators can struggle, primarily because they know what is possible and are always on the lookout for what else is out there. This can become overwhelming for staff who soon become jaded and tired with the next announcement of change. Death by innovation is the likely outcome.

WORKING WITH INNOVATORS

From our experience, we know that it is important to develop a strategy around the Innovators to ensure that they do not get in the way of the development of good practice and that they do not attempt to overlay too many initiatives on top of the existing one. Innovators are extremely passionate people and will constantly be in search of new ideas, whilst their peers will still be reeling from the last change. It can be helpful to acknowledge their role and to talk to them about the importance of letting things settle before introducing other initiatives. Talking to them about the need to allow experimentation and the stages of implementation may be useful. Aside from this, it can be important to help them identify the change agents beneath them and to encourage them to hand over aspects of implementation to others. Having an implementation that is representative of the school community will assist this process – especially when the Innovators occupy positions of power and have trouble letting go.

Early Adopters

Early Adopters are a committed group of people who are open to new ideas, particularly when those new ideas have a potential to make a difference within their area of work. They are often enthusiastic and leading practitioners who look for opportunities to make a difference to their workplace and to their practice. They will give something a try and see effort as an investment, provided there appears to be merit in it. If they see there is support and that outcomes are visible and measurable, they will have a go. They are prepared to take risks, but are also results-orientated and will not adopt a new idea unless it makes sense. They also need acknowledgement for their efforts, as they will give 110 per cent.

This group are admired and respected by others in their workplace, who will be watching closely, and so become the role models for the innovation. The respect this group is held in is important in overcoming the lack of respect that Innovators may experience with the majority of staff. Early Adopters help to decrease the level of uncertainty that new ideas raise, by adopting them, sharing their successes with other members of staff, and minimising the risk to others being asked to adopt the change initiative.

This group will be among the first to attend professional development in restorative practice, to start practice experimentation and to share what they have learnt. After a period of experimentation, the Early Adopters will emerge as the leaders and change agents within their workplace and within the field, as their credibility and ability to make sense of practice will resonate with others. They are also routinely able to translate ideas into layman's terms to assist with practice refinement. A high level of practice competency and emotional literacy is a necessity for this group, as they need to lead by example and model the very skills they are asking others to adopt. Early Adopters are more likely to be people who embrace the restorative philosophy and model the very skills that we are asking others to adopt. Hopkins (2006) suggests that they will work *with* people rather than doing things *to* or *for* them (see also Wachtel and McCold 2000); they will be reflective practitioners, empower others, model working relationally, be accountable and have empathy and compassion for others – all essential skills for change agents. It is also helpful if these people already occupy positions of some weight within the school discipline structures such as faculty heads, year/house leaders or senior teachers; or are those that are empowered by their leaders and supported in the implementation.

WORKING WITH EARLY ADOPTERS

Early Adopters promote innovation through face-to-face contact, both with the Innovators and their colleagues. They will be the ones best placed to deliver peer education once others have introduced the school to the concept of restorative practice. They are the true internal change agents.

It is important to create opportunities for experimentation and permit the Early Adopters to practise in relative safety. Start small and signal to staff that it is a trial phase to be reviewed and adapted to the relative implementation setting. Many schools have used action research to help refine the experimentation phase. Because the Early Adopters are trialling something that is new and challenging, it will be necessary to provide networking and support opportunities for them during the experimentation phase. This will require opportunities for feedback and ongoing dialogue both within the school setting and externally, providing opportunities for practitioners from outside the school system to discuss issues with others at different stages on their journeys. In Australia and New Zealand, regular professional development and networking groups have greatly assisted implementation and keeping the spirits of those involved high. Forums such as these also help facilitate feedback, acknowledge best practice, practice concerns and ongoing professional development, and enable leaders to emerge who will ultimately take practice to another level.

Early Majority

The Early Majority represent 34 per cent of staff in any change initiative (Rogers 2003). They are pragmatists with good will – the type that in a group meeting will agree in principle with the idea (if it makes sense), but they won't be the ones to implement a new initiative, not without first seeing solid evidence that it works. They will neither oppose nor openly support a new idea in the early phases of implementation. They will deliberate for some time before giving an idea a go, and have a tendency to look for easy solutions rather than put themselves out on a limb. This group may be among the quiet achievers, getting on with their work, but will seldom be among the opinion leaders within a group. A staff member within this group may be seen as hindering the change process, because they are not putting strategies into practice simply because they have been told to do so. The Early Majority will follow, but they seldom lead from the front. They need to see restorative practice in action, proof that it works, and that it is practical for them to use. They are the ones who will be influenced by observing and/ or participating in a conference, mini-conference or 'chat' and by observing the actions from colleagues that they otherwise respect and who have credibility within the school/system. 'Most people depend mainly upon a subjective evaluation of an innovation that is conveyed to them from other individuals like themselves who have already adopted the innovation' (Rogers 1994, pp.18–19).

WORKING WITH THE EARLY MAJORITY

Ongoing internal professional dialogue and opportunities to be involved are necessary at this stage. Articles and stories about practice that has worked in other schools will be especially useful, particularly once their interest is triggered. It can help to have a folder of articles and stories ready that you can hand out to colleagues who start to show an interest, or put articles up on the school intranet. You can ask them to read and come back to you with their thoughts to continue the discussion.

Once they put their toes in the water, provide strong support for this group through mentoring and coaching from on-the-ground experienced practitioners and opportunities to send to external training, attend network meetings or visit other schools. This is not a bad strategy, as when something finally makes sense to them and the risk is reduced to a greater degree, they will embrace change. The Early Adopters reduce the risk of innovation for the next group that follows.

Late Majority

The next 34 per cent described by Rogers (2003) are the Late Majority – a conservative, cautious and sceptical group of people who loathe taking risks and doing anything that upsets the status quo. The Late Majority are sticklers for following policy, standards and guidelines and will happily quote these to you when it serves a purpose. They are often challenging to deal with, because they can be vocal and quite obstinate. They are highly influenced by the next group, the Laggards.

The Late Majority only change in response to pressure from the school or department leadership and their peers, that this is how it will be in this school now. They respond best when the uncertainty of a new idea has been removed to such an extent that there is no risk of them failing. Since they are influenced by policy, it is more likely that they will take up new practice when it is clearly defined in policy that is reflective of the restorative paradigm. The Late Majority will adopt the new practice when experimentation to remove the risks, and policy redevelopment to enforce change, has occurred.

Working with the Late Majority

The Late Majority needs trustworthy information about restorative practice. They need to be convinced by those that they respect and credible others (internal and external) that this works and they can put it into practice without much risk. Networking forums that hear from both external leaders in the field and internal change agents will help to catch the attention of this group. Ideally, networking sessions will provide a balance of new material, sharing from everyone about their success stories and their challenges, and the free exchange of information to assist one another. Any one or a combination of sources is likely to capture the attention of this group in a credible way. If visits to other schools are being arranged, consider taking an influential Late Majority adopter with you.

Experimentation and refinement of practice will also increase the convenience and ease of use. Helping others make sense of what they have to do, having the questions on laminated cards that they carry with them or attach in a prominent position will all help in the early stages as well as adapting practice to deal with a range of scenarios: for example, staff meetings that practice how to have a conversation with a small group misbehaving on the playground, with someone who is non-compliant in the classroom, with parents, or with a bully.

Finally, there are two other strategies that will legitimise restorative practice in the eyes of the Late Majority group. The first is to discuss what is *not* working, just as much as we discuss what *is* working with the new initiative, whilst the second is to ensure alignment of school policy and procedures with the restorative paradigm. As one of the pioneers in the field of restorative justice, Howard Zehr (2004), has stated, we need to talk about the 'bullfrog' (what hasn't worked) stories, just as much as we talk about the 'butterfly' (what has worked) stories. We need to respond to criticism raised by the Late Majority and the last group of sceptics, referred to by Rogers (2003) as the Laggards, to remove uncertainty and risk, refine practice and address unspoken concerns about the impact of restorative practice. We need to be vigorous in our review of practice and open about what hasn't worked so well. Only when this happens can we refine practice and develop better practitioners.

Once we are convinced that restorative practice supports school improvement, we need to re-align policy and procedure so that all staff are obliged to follow. This will be particularly important for the Late Majority and Laggards who need a degree of pressure to enable that shift. Properly worked-through policy that involves staff, students and parents in the process will provide an air of legitimacy and the knowledge that 'this is not going away'! At this point, you might think, why not undertake policy change first and avoid such problems in the first place; however, it is our opinion that policy change can only come *after a time of experimentation* and after it makes sense. Policy change too early will evoke resistance, as there is a sense of being told what to do. You cannot force people on board with policy change that is not yet backed up with practice that makes sense. This is one of the primary reasons for change failure that we will discuss in more detail later in this section.

Laggards

> The sceptics are just waiting for a reason to NOT come on board. They are waiting for an excuse and as soon as one of your plans does not go smoothly they will jump on the opportunity to spread dissent amongst the ranks. Some of those who were just about climbing on board may now start to jump ship and it will be even harder to get them back. (Ferris 2003, p.2)

Laggards are often seen as that cynical group of staff who spend their time undermining and blocking change processes. We all know who they are! Rogers (2003) states that they may be very traditional, in which case they are suspicious of innovation; or they may be isolates who lack the social networks to build an awareness of the benefits of the new innovation. Laggards take time to change and evoke a strong urge in others to force change with comments such as 'you are either with us or against us' or 'if you don't like it, move on'.

One thing to remember about the Laggards is that their resistance is completely rational or habitual for them. They have a reason for being cynical it and may fall into any of the following categories:

- waiting for retirement or a better opportunity

- needing to move on, but fearful of making the change

- feeling unsupported by the organisation in the past

- having seen one too many initiatives come and go

- having been overlooked for promotion and being angry about the fact that they have more experience

- being emotionally wounded in some way.

We find that Laggards may be either active or passive in their resistance and may be situational or persistent laggards, and that it is important to differentiate between the two.

SITUATIONAL LAGGARDS

Situational Laggards are often misdiagnosed resisters who become blockers of change due to inept change management. They actively resist initiatives that do not make sense, when their concerns are not heard, or when change has been poorly implemented. It could be that they have been impacted by the initiative or can see a better way. This type of resister can provide important information about how you can do things differently, as Heath and Heath (2010, pp.3–16) distinguish:

- what looks like a people problem is often a situational problem

- what looks like laziness is often exhaustion, and

- if you want people to change, you must provide crystal-clear direction.

WORKING WITH SITUATIONAL LAGGARDS

Engaging Situational Laggards in dialogue, taking their concerns seriously and involving them in the change process can provide important information about what is working and not working in the change initiative. It is essential to involve them in the change process and provide regular opportunities for two-way communication. The challenge with managing Situational Laggards is that they have quite often attempted to express their concerns only to be ignored or put off. The risk is that by the time those managing the change realise the error of their ways, this Situational Laggard has either moved on or has become a Persistent Laggard. Nine times out of ten you will have lost them in the intervening time, with the old adage that in times of mismanagement you lose your best people, not the ones you would wish gone.

PERSISTENT LAGGARDS

Persistent Laggards have a tendency to be opposed to any initiative that they have not thought of themselves. They will hold out until the end hoping that the new idea will soon be forgotten. After all, they are among a group of people who have become cynical about change processes and have seen plenty of new ideas come and go. Persistent Laggards have a tendency to hang out together in staffrooms or in particular faculties and will be vocal in their objections to any new idea. They are suspicious of Innovators and Early Adopters and are sceptical of the Early Majority who look like they are sitting on the fence, although have some sympathy with the Late Majority who are a little opposed to risk-taking themselves.

Working with Persistent Laggards

It is *not* a good idea to try to influence these people by sending an Innovator into their 'patch' to engage them in a debate about the relative advantages of the restorative approach. John Braithwaite (2007) offers some fabulous insight on this in his work with warring tribal groups and bullies. Often the way to deal with it is by increasing your circle of influence so you initially work with those who are aligned with the cause. You empower them to resist the approach of the warlord, the bully or, in our case, the Persistent Laggard. You create alternative experiences that are different from the one painted by the Persistent Laggard or the bully. You then work with the next layer and so forth, peeling the layers of the onion away, until the field of influence that the main aggressor or resister had is so reduced that their destructive powers are all but gone. At this stage they will either come on board or move on.

There is also a time and place where both Situational and Persistent Laggards may need to be confronted about their behaviour, especially when they are resistant as the result of being passed over for opportunities and promotion or are underperforming. Whatever the situation, it will need to be addressed in a firm, fair and restorative way. Whilst challenging, managing performance in a restorative or relational way will benefit all parties affected and save a lot of heartache in the long term, provided it is managed well, as this next case study attests.

Case Study: From Laggard to Early Adopter

Pamela and Anne were two primary school teachers in a challenging school environment. Both had different issues that had a major impact on the school environment, the students in their class, parents, colleagues and community members. Pamela screamed at her class a lot, was easily stressed and very 'slippery' in terms of handing in her programmes for the year. In fact, on inquiry, it was found that she hadn't done this for several years, always providing an excuse and gaining extension after extension, until the Executive team had long forgotten the programme and were caught up with other priorities. There was no accountability and because Pamela was so challenging to deal with, the school adopted the attitude that there was little they could do, but hope she moved on. The trouble was, Pamela had been there longer than anyone else.

Anne was different. She was petulant, easily angered, and frequently inappropriate with peers and community members – although a brilliant teacher by all accounts. Everyone around her walked on eggshells. There was a constant joke on whether the staffroom was clear to enter in terms of Anne's behaviour. Anne was well defended and was very difficult to deal with. Most people gave her a wide berth. Because she was so unpredictable it made people far more accepting of Pamela's behaviour, because at least she didn't yell at them.

The more relational and responsive the school became to working with students, each other and the community, the more unpalatable the behaviour of these two staff members became. It was time for the leader of the school to take action and apply both pressure to lift their standard and the support to make the change. It was initially thought that both would need to be put on performance management plans. Each in turn was called in to speak with the principal and was dealt with in a restorative manner. Their behaviour was called to account, whilst their worth as teachers was acknowledged. Demands were placed on both of them in the areas where they had deficits. Pamela was teamed up with a leading teacher to assist with getting the teaching programme in. Dates were set and a review period established. It was not going to go away this time. The screaming in the classroom was raised as a concern and a conversation had to explore what was happening and what could be done differently. Pamela was treated as a partner in the process, but the pressure was on. Anne was advised to seek assistance with managing the fluctuations in moods and ultimately sought professional help. Regular meetings were established to check progress and to assist Anne to make this shift. Over time, the days in which she walked in happy and stayed happy outweighed the bad days.

Five years, on both Pamela and Anne were still at the school, and were considered among the leading teachers. They had immense enthusiasm, had become coordinators for special aspects within the school and were clearly well respected. Laggards are Laggards for a reason and when we tap into that and help them make the change, they can become leading practitioners and advocates for the new systems. Often it is not that they themselves are unwell, but it is a symptom of the system they are working within and they just happen to be expressing it – quite often, very loudly and inappropriately!

Laggards can become your greatest leaders and advocates if you tap into the frustration that they feel about what has happened in the past. It is important that while we don't invest all our time and energy in changing their minds, we must not write them off totally. If we pay attention to their concerns, and hold them to account, they may well become our greatest advocates, and in turn substantially impact the Late Majority.

The more restorative/relational a school becomes, the more urgency there is to align all processes and people to operate restoratively/relationally. Ultimately, the Executive will reach a point where they have to apply both pressure and support for the Laggards to change. At the same time, it starts to become intolerable for those that are unwilling or cannot change to remain within a relational environment. At this point, many choose simply to move on.

The important message here is that change agents, both internal and external, must give careful thought to the processes they use for engagement, so that their energy is spent in a worthwhile manner. Get some 'process' advice if necessary.

How does an understanding of diffusion theory assist implementation?

People adopt things for their own reasons – not for ours. Innovation must make sense for people in order for them to consider adopting it and they will adopt it at different rates. For this reason, we need to plan implementation strategies to match Rogers' (2003) diffusion model categories. A whole school training in one sitting is not the most effective way to proceed as it will only reach or convince some and certainly not others. The Early Majority will need to see it in practice and require assistance to minimise the risk for them, whilst the Late Majority and Laggards will need further reinforcement and professional development down the track.

Those tasked with implementing change and change agents need not only to make the case for change by making the linkages and outlining how restorative practices can make a difference, but also need to convince managers and hierarchies of the need to be strategic. We simply can't expect people to change because we want them to. Take-up by the Innovators and Early Adopters must be regarded as a developmental phase in which the ideology must give way to flexible and practical solutions. It is a time for experimentation and fine-tuning. Flexible options must be developed. Teething problems are normal and a frank discussion about what works and what doesn't is critical, whilst risk-taking is encouraged. *It is essential that funds are made available to sustain the change process beyond this developmental work.* To withdraw funding after one to two years is a grave mistake and in our experience usually results in a failure to develop sustainable practice and a revert to type before it is realised that change must be reinvigorated.

For restorative practice to move more towards mainstream acceptance, we must ensure that it meets and addresses a genuine need; that it does not come at a great risk to the majority; and that RP becomes part of the language and 'the way we do things'.

Finally, it is important to acknowledge that whilst a lot of this may seem daunting, it only takes a 10–20 per cent rate of adoption to reach tipping point (Gladwell 2000; Chan Kim and Mauborgne 2003) – as the Early Majority and Late Majority are influenced by the Innovators and the Early Adopters – but it takes strategic planning to reaching tipping point. We discuss this in detail in the last section of this book.

Chapter 5

Why Change Fails

There are many barriers to change, with the main issue from our experience of working in and with organisations being that too few understand what is required to effectively manage change. It is not too difficult to understand why research estimates that upwards of 70 per cent of change initiatives fail (Zigarmi *et al.* 2006), when we consider the following case.

Case Study: How Change Initiatives Fail

A school had a grand vision for change, developed without consultation with frontline teaching staff. The school senior management team advised staff that change was mooted and the broad direction the school was taking. Even with scant information, for some this change process was both exciting and challenging, involving major reforms and changes in personnel. The changes meant that some staff saw opportunities to develop themselves in ways previously not thought of and, for them, there was a mix of interest and excitement in the process. (You might recognise these as the Early Adopters of change that we referred to in Rogers' (2003) Diffusion Model. These are the very people that need to be nurtured and encouraged to come on board, as they will generally have influence among their peers, who in turn may be concerned about their future, wondering what the impact on them will be.)

Others in this change process opted to be more strategic and made up their minds about whether the future involved them, and what that might mean for them, as information came to hand. (Known as the Early Majority, they were not opposed to change, but at the same time would not buy into it until they had more information and it was safe to do so.)

Others were blissfully unaware of what was happening around them and possibly only wanted to do their jobs, which may already have been burdensome enough. (Known as the Late Majority, they will not engage in change until 50 per cent of their colleagues are on board and it is clearly the way that things are going.)

> The remaining staff were openly or quietly opposed to change. (Whilst often maligned, the Laggards are the most challenging group to shift and, yet, they may simply be disenfranchised Early Adopters.)

So you might see that, unless you have key people on board, the change process is doomed to fail, because it will not address the emotional concerns and needs of those expected to change. It is not difficult to see why this still ongoing change initiative is unlikely to succeed in the manner that the institution has proposed. In fact, at the time of completing this book, many teaching staff had left, been dismissed or retrenched, or action threatened. The school has finally acknowledged that there did appear to be a problem with how change was communicated. To address this, they placed some information about change on the intranet. Now, we will leave it to your imagination as to how successful you think this initiative will be to engage remaining staff.

In the case study, there are many errors, starting with announcing the change as if it was a fait accompli and expecting people to go along with that. The senior management did not engage in real dialogue or hear people's concerns about the process. In fact, as you will see in the section that follows, they did very little to ensure that the change initiative would work. The implementers then made the fundamental error of not valuing input from the Early Adopters, but rather marginalised them. When your best performers turn against you, it is a recipe for disaster, because there is no one to bring the rest of the staff on board, those who have been watching the process and made up their minds not to stick their heads up. Now, at this point, you might think this is an extreme example, but if you reflect on how often this has occurred in your working career, you will perhaps see the point we are highlighting. Put simply, change is difficult unless you know what you are doing.

Major culture change initiatives bring with them interest, excitement, enjoyment for some, and a host of negative affects for others such as distress, fear, anxiety and anger. Will I have a job? What will the requirements be? Will I have to change? How does this impact me? What does it mean in terms of my job satisfaction? Change that does not involve in meaningful dialogue and participation the very people affected by the change is doomed to fail. Without this, those that may have initially been excited by the change will start to doubt the process and turn against the initiative, no matter how much the implementers attempt to sidestep this process. Change is an emotional process.

When we look at the implementation of restorative practice, we are asking implementation teams to change the minds and hearts of school practitioners. We are asking them to shift from a punitive or authoritarian frame to a relational/authoritative way of behaving that we discuss in Section 1 of this book. We are asking them to be genuine, warm and real in front of a class of 20–40 students. Some manage this well, whilst others hide behind a professional façade of 'I am the teacher and they are the students and they will do what they are told.' This is not surprising when we consider the way many of us were schooled and parented. To be a relational educator requires strong relationships with students, colleagues and each other – needing skills that we may not have learned in our own family of origin. These relationships are characterised by healthy dialogue. Put simply, a relational educator understands and values relational pedagogy. Plenty, however, will resist this approach for a range of very valid reasons. Identifying what it takes to engage and reassure people in the change process is critical, otherwise it is likely to fail or be less than effective. As Bridges (1995) states, even good change begins with having to let go of something and the pain of this cannot be underestimated. The reality is, change is hard, takes time and too much of it fails due to a host of reasons that we will outline.

5.1 Kotter's Eight Mistakes and the Consequences

Kotter (2012a) provides eight reasons why change fails and the consequences for an organisation when this happens. In terms of change, he is referring to initiatives that transform or renew an organisation, as is the case with the implementation of restorative practice. An initiative such as this is about changing the hearts and minds of practitioners, something that takes time and careful consideration. The eight mistakes are outlined by Kotter (2012a) as:

- allowing complacency

- failing to develop a guiding coalition

- underestimating the power of a vision
- under-communicating the vision
- permitting obstacles to block the change vision
- failing to create short-term wins
- declaring victory too soon
- neglecting to anchor change.

These are expanded on in Table 5.1. The consequences of this are that:

- change is not implemented well
- synergies are not achieved
- restructuring takes too long and costs too much
- downsizing that often results doesn't fix the problem
- quality initiatives don't get the results that could be achieved
- morale is negatively affected
- the best people leave the organisation
- indirect communication increases, and
- active undermining of change processes occurs.

How often have we heard the saying, 'Oh we tried that, and it didn't work!' Kotter in his extensive body of literature on this topic explains why this is the case. In our modern time-poor, competitive world, time is of the essence, as is the bottom line, and that has affected the business of schools just as much as in organisations and businesses in competition with one another in the private sector. Kotter (2012a) indicates that with awareness of these common errors, they can be mitigated and largely avoided. The key is leadership understanding and know-how to overcome the inertia and resistance to change. As we have already indicated, this is about getting people on board, rather than getting them offside or expecting them to walk because we have instructed them to do so.

Table 5.1 Eight mistakes in the change process (adapted from Kotter 1995, 2012a)

The steps	Reason for failure at each step
1. Allowing complacency	• not establishing a great enough sense of urgency – making a clear statement that doing things the way we do them is no longer acceptable • not understanding or creating the need for change – why a change initiative is required • not having the right person in charge to lead the change initiative or understanding that change requires a particular skill-set
2. Failing to build a powerful guiding coalition	• not creating a powerful enough coalition early in the change process to help drive the change • relying on one or two people to lead the change initiative • key people in critical positions are not on board and/or are not given time to develop a change vision and how to achieve this • underestimating the challenges of the change initiative • lacking strong leadership from above to help drive the change
3. Failing to develop a vision for change	• lacking a clear, simple-to-understand and big enough vision for change • failing to adjust the vision as the change process is implemented – potentially altering the direction of change

4. Failing to communicate the vision for buy-in	• failing to lead by example and to 'walk the talk' – behaviour that is inconsistent with the change initiative • failing to incorporate the change initiative into ongoing communication and correspondence • allowing processes to remain in place when found to be inconsistent with the change initiative • failing to treat people affected by the change process fairly • failing to indicate whether proposed solutions align with the change initiative
5. Failing to empower others to act on the vision and to remove barriers	• failing to confront and remove obstacles to the new vision • allowing processes to remain in place which are inconsistent with the change initiative • leaders who refuse to change and/or make demands that are inconsistent with the change initiative • failing to empower others or to hear the creative ideas that change processes generate
6. Failing to plan for and generate short-term wins	• not systematically planning for and creating short-term wins • no evidence of tangible change within 12–24 months
7. Declaring victory too soon	• urgency of change not intense • failing to understand that renewal efforts take years rather than months or a one-off session
8. Failing to anchor the new approaches into the culture of the school – making it stick	• not anchoring change in the organisation's culture, 'the way we do things around here' • removing the pressure for change before change is embedded • not demonstrating how the change initiative has had a positive impact • failing to employ people that personify the change initiative

Kotter's (2012a) work goes to the heart of what we have expressed throughout this book. If restorative practice was just another programme that you pulled off the shelf for a term or two, then little of this would matter. Instead, restorative practice has the potential to make a whole lot of difference to the culture of schools and the nature of relationships within the school community. In fact, without this, practice would be seen as little more than a behaviour management tool instead of *the way we do things around here*. To achieve this, implementers, change agents and external professional development providers need to understand the nature of change, the difficulties around this and why people resist this change.

5.2 Zigarmi *et al.*'s Fifteen Mistakes

Where Kotter (1995, 2012a) places an emphasis on the eight mistakes implementers of change make, Zigarmi *et al.* (2006) provide a list of 15 predictable reasons for why change efforts fail, many of which overlap with Kotter's (2012a) understanding of this process. In this case, we have outlined how this looks in terms of the implementation of restorative practice.

1. People leading the change think that announcing the change is implementation

This is a common problem with restorative practice in schools, where leaders who may be enthusiastic (perhaps Innovators themselves) make an announcement that this is what is going to happen, often without exposing the whole staff to the principles and practice; or conducting a one-day session and expecting staff to implement without additional support or dialogue. Of course, in most instances this practice is less than successful, with perhaps only a handful of staff picking the new ideas up and putting them into practice. Whole school change will not be possible without ongoing dialogue and a strategic approach to managing the change process. It takes years to successfully embed practice and to bring about cultural change. As Kotter (1995) indicates, this is one of the major reasons why change fails, because organisations underestimate the time needed to bring about change and underestimate the effort required.

2. People's concerns with change are not surfaced and addressed

As we have discussed, ignore the resisters at your peril! We can learn from them and need to involve them in differing ways. It is important to listen to people, to establish what their concerns are and to sufficiently support people in their practice development. One such issue raised is always around time. The time that it takes to learn, develop and modify practice is real. Whilst this is an investment that will ultimately save time down the track, it does take time. In order to manage this, it is important that staff are supported in making this change, that if they are expected to put the practices in place then they are supported in doing so.

3. Those asked to change are not involved in planning

How often have you been part of a change process where you have been told to do something different, but have no say in the process? Or worse still, you find problems in the process, but your feedback is not heard or taken on board. In Section 3 we discuss the need for implementation teams that are representative of the school and seek to involve a good cross-section of people and representatives from each group.

4. The need for change is not communicated

As Kotter (1995, 2012a) indicates, the first step towards change is to create a sense of urgency in which it is clear why the implementation of restorative practices is necessary. There has to be something in it for people to adopt new practice, especially practice that may fundamentally challenge the way they have done things. In this case, we discuss the need for building the case for change, so the imperative is understood and provides a catalyst for change. This aligns neatly with Kotter's (1995) step of generating and communicating short-term wins that will be discussed in Section 3 of this book.

5. Lack of shared vision

A clear picture of what you are working towards is required to share this dream. As the person tasked with implementation in your school, do you understand what you are working towards and how to take others along on this journey? Beyond the school vision for the future, it is about a clear vision for change in terms of how restorative practice will assist your school to improve the imperatives that have been identified; how it underpins the vision.

6. Change leadership fails to include adopters, resisters and informal leaders

When considering the alignment with Kotter's (1995) steps for change, this is about failing to sufficiently spread the field of influence to pick up those affected by the implementation of restorative practice. This includes those in influential positions such as year-level heads, heads of house, vice/deputy principals, principals/heads, team leaders, those at the coalface, and those who are firmly against it. It is important to build a powerful guiding coalition (Kotter 1995) in order to support the implementation of restorative practice.

7. Lack of experimentation and adaptation

This is believing that a one-size-fits-all implementation approach works and there is no need for experimentation. What we know is that the practices work throughout the world in a range of cultural settings, although it is important to understand the intricacies of working in each setting and to adapt practice accordingly. Rogers (2003) reminds us that an innovation will not be adopted unless it can be 're-invented' (p.180) to suit the setting. At the same time, this can be a trap in the sense that schools believe that their environment is unique compared with other school environments and start changing the nature of the practice so much that the integrity is lost. How practice is interpreted is something that requires ongoing dialogue and referral back to the intent of this work. Are we being restorative or is this simply another big stick in the form of something else – punishment thinly disguised as a restorative process?

8. Lack of alignment of traditional/existing systems with innovation

Operating alongside or over the top of traditional values without seeking an alignment between restorative practice and the old way of doing things (down the track) will eventually cause a problem and lead to a disconnect between what we say we do and what we actually do in practice. Still caning or using other punishments, following a successful restorative process, will ultimately lead to someone asking, 'Why we still doing this?' This will require a review of the whole school discipline process to ensure that the primary aim is to bring about learning, develop responsible behaviours and to stop the unhelpful behaviours, rather than punishing for the sake of punishing, *because that is the way we have always done things.*

9. Failure to focus and prioritise: 'death by a thousand initiatives'

As we like to put it – *innovation gone mad!* A common problem for schools who have an abundance of 'off-the-shelf' initiatives to choose from is how to embed a new programme before embarking on the next new one. Schools are usually implementing a range of initiatives and seeking to implement something different each term or semester. In the end, staff become reluctant to adopt any new practice because, in reality, they know that this 'fad' will pass and before long they will be required to implement something else. Believe us – we have seen and experienced way too much of this!

In many cases it is about making a clear case for change and how the initiatives are aligned and relate to the whole, rather than being seen as separate initiatives with no interconnecting aspects. Schools that are effective in working restoratively implement a range of initiatives in order to develop the whole school social, emotional and academic learning environment, but they are also successful in explaining how all three aspects (as we have discussed in Section 1) are critical to the overall school success and the vision for change.

10. People not enabled to develop new skills

In this case, people are told they will be implementing restorative practice after being exposed to a one-day or shorter awareness-raising session (often referred to as an introduction to restorative practice). We have delivered many of these with the intent of informing and raising awareness, only to hear schools say they have been 'trained'. Another error is that the provision for training and networking is not built into the budget, or access to training is restricted to certain people who may not be influential in the development of practice. When pushing for whole school change, it is critical to target Early Adopters who are expected to put the new ideas into practice and influence others.

11. Leaders who are not credible and give mixed messages

It is vital that we are congruent in what we do and say (Hopkins 2004; Kotter 1995). Leaders that expect one thing and do something completely different will lose credibility and greatly affect the change management process. This goes as far as the way leaders talk to staff and deal with difficulties within the school, at all levels. We discuss the importance of leadership at the end of this section of the book.

12. Progress is not measured

The implementation of restorative practice will soon fail if people don't know what the purpose of the change initiative is or what the school is hoping to achieve. Not knowing what we are trying to achieve or what the progress markers are will contribute to failing to celebrate the small wins and big changes along the way. To do this, it is critical that we gather and analyse that data along the way.

13. People are not held accountable for the implementation

All too often, schools instruct staff that this is the way they are going to do things, without holding anyone to account in the process. If there is a lack of leadership and a team responsible for the implementation of sustainable practice, the implementation will fail.

14. A failure to respect and understand the culture in which you are seeking to implement the innovation

It is important to understand the culture of the school before you start the change process. Is the school deeply traditional with long-standing ways of doing business that will be hard to unfreeze? Is it a new school just beginning to create its preferred culture? Is it a school with a large multi-cultural population where punishments seem pointless? Is it a school that is already relational in its approach to problem-solving? Is it a school with a history of inadequate leadership? It is important to know what the scale of the change might need to be. This is something that is all too often ignored as implementers get frustrated with why things haven't changed in the way they had hoped. The other aspect that affects change tremendously is where the relationships amongst staff and between staff and management are not aligned with the restorative philosophy. People don't take kindly to being expected to do things one way and being treated in a way that is completely contrary to this.

15. Other options are not explored in the experimentation and development phase

Change requires experimentation and adaptation of practice to individual settings, such as working with students with special needs or younger students. We talk about the need to develop specific adaptations in Section 3 of this book. Staff must be provided with the opportunity to experiment and to discuss what is working and not working in terms of the application of this practice. This requires a commitment to ongoing dialogue about the implementation of restorative practice, just as one would need to do around raising literacy and numeracy standards.

Chapter 6

Change is an
Emotional Process

Just as 'change is inevitable: so is resistance to change' (Moorhead and Griffin 1998, p.555). Imagine yourself as the educator in the classroom doing your best to make a difference. You work up front all day giving your best to your students, you prepare your classes, you review your students' work and give them feedback, you manage the dynamics of your class and any challenging behaviours, you attend professional learning opportunities and keep abreast of change and what is required of you. You already give more than is required, because that is what it takes to do your job well. Then, along comes a member of the leadership team to announce yet another change process. This is the third initiative of the year and you are now starting to wonder what happened to the last two initiatives that you were expected to put into place, but appear to have dropped off the agenda through lack of commitment and resourcing. *Sound familiar?*

Now step back into your shoes as the implementer of this change. You are excited about this, you know the implementation of restorative practice will make a difference and you are driven to do something about it. As you excitedly share this with your colleagues, you watch the faces change, people start shuffling in their seats and you hear the disgruntlement. By the end of the session, your emotions have gone from a high – the affect of interest-excitement and enjoyment-joy – to feeling completely deflated as you realise the enormity of the task. Or perhaps you are more resolute and instruct them that this is going to happen and they'd better get with it or leave! You may well laugh at the absurdity of the process or wince at this point, because you know this feeling all too well. In fact, we could have just evoked a shame response, because you can hear your own words to staff. We have all experienced this in different ways. Change evokes a host of emotions, both within those that need to embrace the change and within those that are required to implement change. This needs to be understood and managed well if change is to be successful.

6.1 The Emotional Stages

'Resistance increases the more people sense that they cannot influence what is happening to them' (Zigarmi and Hoekstra 2006, p.226). As we have discussed so far, change is an emotional process and generally fails when we do not take this into account and bring the very people expected to change on board. The other reason for failure is failing to communicate what is required and supporting people in this process. The following discussion examines the nature of resistance and denial that can be expected in any change process. No matter how well change is implemented, this is a common phenomenon that needs to be managed. It is also recognised that not everyone is able or willing to go through yet another change initiative. It is often at this time that people may choose to move on or leave an occupation, which is not a bad thing if their heart is not in it.

Adams, Hayes and Hopson (1976) provide a diagrammatic view of the emotional stages that people go through in any change transition process and how their sense of competence is affected by change (Figure 6.1).

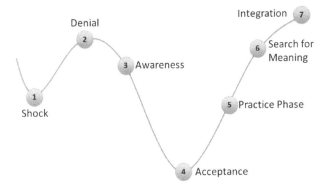

Figure 6.1 The transition curve (adapted from Adams, Hayes and Hopson 1976)

The transition curve examines the impact of a person's personal sense of competence over time during the transition process. In the beginning, the announcement of a change initiative may throw someone into a state of *shock* (1 in Figure 6.1) or certainly result in an impediment to interest and excitement. This may lead to a range of responses such as fight, flight, despair or paralysis. At the same time, someone's competence as a practitioner may be challenged.

Following this initial state of shock, those affected by the change may enter into a form of *denial* (2), where a false sense of competence is evoked ('this doesn't apply to me' – or, 'if I stand very still, this change won't impact on me'). With a little time and space, people may start to accept that change is necessary and develop *awareness* (3) of their own competence. The next stage is one of *acceptance* (4) that this is necessary and that 'the way we do things is changing around here'. At this stage, competence is at a rock-bottom level, as people are left wondering if they have a role to play in the new world. Let's look at an example to see how this can play out in reality.

Case Study: The Transition Curve in Practice

A teacher received an ill-timed email on a Friday afternoon indicating that their teaching hours were being reduced. The email questioned their competency to teach in their chosen subject area. The teacher reacted badly to the news, immediately going into a state of shock, very quickly followed with an emotional outburst to the sender of the email. As Kelly (2012) indicates, this extreme state of distress then led to a shame response and instant 'attack other' in the form of a hurried email response back. In emotional or affect terms, the news was an immediate impediment to the teacher feeling good about themselves and challenged their sense of professional competence. The teacher then cycled through Adams *et al.*'s (1976) stage 2 of denial, inflating their experience to prove competency and to feel better about themselves, before reaching a place of awareness and understanding that standards were changing and there were new requirements to teach in that area. The transition in this case took a week. From this place, the teacher had a choice of whether to demonstrate and prove their competence, up-skill, accept the decision, or opt out of teaching altogether.

In reality, the whole situation could have been handled differently right from the start, by communicating the altered requirements and indicating that conversations would start happening to assist staff to either meet the requirements or to examine alternative options. When we consider the needs of people in the change process, information communicated to all staff would go part way to raising awareness of the need/reason for reason for change and perhaps lessen the shock and denial. An effective process does not necessarily mean that someone would not have reacted the same way, because it fundamentally challenges our professional sense of self. Awareness of this will help those of you tasked with change to catch the responses and to see them for what they are. However, we advise against this form of hit-and-run type of correspondence in the first place as it is hardly relational or restorative!

Over time, as we start to accept the change initiative, we then have an opportunity to experiment, test out new approaches and increase our confidence at a competence level. This is referred to by Adams *et al.* (1976), as the *experimentation praxis* which we have referred to as *practice phase* (5). With feedback, this allows for those affected by the change to *search for new meanings* (6), which is the phase where people develop and test out new skills. They create new understandings of their competence level, especially as they understand how things work – something that was completely missing in the cited example. The height of competence is achieved when new skills and behaviours are *integrated* (7) into practice, which then can deliver a sense of deep satisfaction from developing new skills and perhaps achieving better outcomes.

When one considers that the implementation of restorative practice fundamentally challenges the hearts and minds of individuals, then it is not surprising that it can evoke in some the emotional response that we are describing. This does not mean that change should be avoided, rather that we need to be aware that change evokes a range of responses in people. This is especially the case when staff come to the realisation that the old punitive based models of classroom management and behaviour change are ineffective. Of course, this will be met with shock, plummeting sense of competence and a sense of, for some, 'how dare you challenge my competence'. This is why it is so important to build the case for change that we discuss later, so that you alleviate a lot of the initial heartache for people. A case for change, a clear vision and intensive skill development will all help this process. To not do so is to set the change initiative up for failure.

6.2 The Blueprint for Emotional Connection

When we consider that change evokes a host of sometimes positive, but mostly negative emotions, then we need to consider what people need in this process to ensure they develop a healthy connection with one another, instead of their relationships needlessly suffering. As we have discussed earlier in this book, healthy relationships within the school between staff, students and staff, parents and teachers and the leadership team are essential. Kelly (2012) outlines his Blueprint for Healthy Emotional Connection that is predicated on the need for human beings to:

1. work together to create positive feelings and foster them as much as possible

2. work together to do everything possible to reduce or eliminate negative feelings

3. avoid hiding feelings from the other in order to better carry out 1 and 2, and

4. share in developing the power and skills necessary to do 1–3 to the fullest.

When we consider change management and how tough it can be, we want to create and foster positive feelings by creating and acknowledging the short-term wins along the way. We need to be in regular dialogue about what is getting us down, what is not working or not going so well. We need permission to be able to share this and to know that the environment in which we work is prepared to hear us. Finally, we need to continually develop the skills and ability to be able to work together and to acknowledge it isn't always easy, especially in the midst of change. An important aspect of this is allowing people the space to air their concerns.

6.3 What Concerns do People Have?

A US Department of Education Project (cited in Blanchard 2006) cited six sequential and predictable concerns that people need addressed in the adoption of change. These concerns were about: quality information; how change will affect them personally; what are the sequential stages of implementation (who will do what, when); what impact will this have and will it make a difference; who else will be involved; and how can we refine the change process to continually improve.

People will naturally be resistant if they feel their concerns are not addressed. Who is resistant will change in response to the proposed change initiative and how it is implemented. An Early Adopter of restorative practice, for example, can become resistant to further change if the process has not been well resourced or supported along the way, or if they feel that the effort that it takes to keep it going is left to them. Addressing these concerns in a strategic way, as outlined in Section 3 of this book, will help manage the resistance to change, as will addressing the concerns that people share. We discuss each of these concerns in more detail here.

Information concerns

People require the same information as was needed by those that made the initial decision to adopt restorative practice. Consider that when a principal decides that RP is exactly what the school needs, do the rest of the school have information about what the problem is that needs addressing, and how this initiative will assist in resolving that problem? In the absence of quality information, staff will fill in the gaps themselves. People need answers to the following questions:

1. What is the change?

2. Why is it needed?

3. What is wrong with the way things are now?

4. How do we know this works?

5. Is it evidence-based?

6. How much and how fast does the organisation need to change?

This will all help to build awareness of the reason for change and the need for everyone to get on board. This is a typical outline for the introduction to restorative practice, which seeks to inform and raise awareness.

Personal concerns

People want to know how the change will affect them and whether they have the skills and resources to implement the change. It is critical at this stage that their concerns are taken seriously and they feel heard:

1. How will the change impact me personally?
2. What's in it for me?
3. How will I find the time to implement change?
4. Will I have to learn new skills?

As Adams *et al.* (1976) indicated, a person's self-perception of their competence can plummet at the beginning and in the midst of a change initiative.

Implementation concerns

People need to know how the implementation will be rolled out. This includes the need for information about the stages of implementation, who will be working on this and what it all means. In the early stages of buy-in, the detail of the change process is unlikely to be developed, but as staff become engaged in the process, this is the ideal time to call for volunteers, or to ask key people to be involved, in order to develop the implementation plan. This then needs to be communicated clearly to all staff, so that they have the information that is required and know who is doing what.

Impact concerns

Change has an impact on people. At every step towards becoming a restorative school, people will be required to adapt or align practice and processes to a restorative and relational way of working.

People need to know how change will impact them and, for some, this will mean making a decision that this is not the place for them and they may opt to move on. As Blanchard (2006) states, if the first three concerns around information, implementation and how change affects them personally are in place, they will likely be sold on the process of change and stay. Regardless, they will be in a position to make an informed decision about their level of buy-in or to opt out with good grace and go. This in itself is not necessarily a bad thing, as many of us can recall a leaving that was not potentially planned, but turned out to be the best thing we could have done.

Collaboration concerns

With buy-in, people start asking how they can be involved and who else needs to be involved. You might hear the call for parents and students to be informed and involved; for relief staff to be part of the process; and potentially, more broadly, people within the system and within the community engaged. At this stage, the process makes sense to people, they can see the benefit and want this message communicated to others. The leadership team may visit other schools, involve feeder schools, talk to others within the system or may present at related conferences.

Refinement concerns

Refinement is about the continual change process and attention to the detail of quality and sustainable practice. At this stage, implementation will be well embedded and there will be an emerging concern about how change will be sustained and how to keep it alive within the school. This includes planning for new staff, changes to staffing and for a new cohort of students. Schools that develop sustainable practice have a long-term plan for ongoing professional development of staff and for bringing new staff on board.

Addressing the above information, personal, implementation, impact, collaboration and refinement concerns is critical in terms of reducing resistance and managing the anxiety and fear in the change process. Another critical area is indicating how long cultural change is likely to take and allowing people time to experiment and develop new skills, behaviours and attitudes to ensure quality practice development. People have a need for quality information on and during the change process. They need to know how change will affect them personally; what the sequential stages of implementation are (who will do what, when); what impact it will have and how will it make a difference; who will be involved; and what the process of improvement is.

6.4 Denial

Change takes time and people change in their own good time. We estimate that the implementation of restorative practice takes anywhere between three and five years, and even longer in secondary schools. In fact, if schools are serious, the job is never done. Just as people need their concerns addressed, we need to understand that people change at different rates (see the adopter categories at the beginning of this section) and that cultural change takes time. Ferris (2003) states that 'it is imperative that those taking the longest are given sufficient time to come on board. They should not be abandoned just because the majority are already there, or this could be your downfall' (p.2).

It is completely normal for people to progress through the following phases (Ferris 2003, p.2):

1. *Denial.* 'It is just another fad and it simply won't happen.'

2. *Resistance.* 'I haven't got the time and anyway, we have always done things this way.'

3. *Exploration.* 'OK – maybe I'll listen, but what is in it for me?'

4. *Commitment.* 'I believe in this and I am with you.'

We will focus on two key aspects: *denial* and *resistance*.

Denial and resistance are normal responses in the face of change, and even though expected, cause a lot of frustration to those implementing innovations. Affect theory, personality development, learning styles and the theory of discounting can all help to develop our understanding of how people adopt change at different rates. It is a mix of how change is implemented, what is happening for the person at the time, past experiences, how they learn and the nature of the environment they are working within. We have all been resistant to change at times. Take for example the adoption of new technology and you might recall a reluctance to embrace the latest change. We may discount the need to embrace the change at a number of levels.

Illsley Clarke and Dawson (1998) describe how people have a tendency to discount when confronted with a problem. Discounting is treating a situation as less significant than it really is and can occur at four levels:

1. *Existence.* What problem? I don't see a problem.

2. *Significance.* There is a problem but it's not serious.

3. *Change possibilities.* There is a problem, it is significant but nothing can be done.

4. *Personal abilities.* There is a problem and it is significant, something needs to be done, but I don't know what to do.

Case Study: Discounting in Action

Let's take the example of bullying.

At level 1 (problem existence): I walk past a bunch of older boys interacting with a younger boy and don't even notice that the younger child is upset.

At level 2 (problem significance): I see the younger child is upset and say, 'It will be good for him – he needs to toughen up.'

At level 3 (change possibilities): I walk past the boys, see the younger child is upset, think it's serious but say, 'What can you do, boys will be boys.'

At level 4 (personal abilities): I walk past the boys, see what is happening, know it is serious, know something could be done but say, 'I hate conflict and don't know what to say to stop it.'

Identifying the level of discount is important in terms of knowing how much energy to put into changing the underlying belief pattern. It is much harder to work with people discounting at levels 1 and 2, where they cannot see a problem or fail to take the need for change seriously, than it is for those who believe that there are no solutions to the problem or who feel powerless to make a difference at levels 3 and 4. In the case of the latter, the provision of solutions or ways to work with the problems will address the concerns informing the discounting of the issue.

Thankfully, within schools, the latter two levels are among the most common forms of discounting, where educators are quick to identify and blame parents, their students/pupils, society and the media for the problems that they face, forming a mistaken belief that there is no solution or they are powerless to make a difference. We in turn cannot discount that what they are saying is not serious or not real for them. We need to find ways to work with this if we are to start altering the belief patterns. Information and strategies based around engagement will mostly address this problem at the third and fourth level. There is a fifth option, which is to not discount at any level. This response requires facing the problem or situation up front and empowering all those involved to address it effectively.

Whilst there are many reasons why people discount, one of them is the emotional discomfort that they experience. The Compass of Shame (Nathanson 1992) provides a further understanding of the nature of denial. There are a cluster or family of behaviours called Avoidance that individuals use to manage intense feelings of shame and disconnection. Denial is a form of saying 'no', a defence mechanism whereby the 'denial implies refusal of anything asked for or desired, the assertion that something is untrue, the contradiction of the existence or the reality of a thing' (Nathanson 1992, p.337). Disavowal is a form of denial, where one cannot comprehend certain information because it triggers unwanted affect. In another explanation for denial behaviours, Nathanson (1992) states that 'we can protect ourselves by guarding the perimeters of our personal world; by making sure there is nothing within them that will embarrass us; or by distracting people so that they will forget that they were interested in what may lie within' (p.339). When we feel uncomfortable, we want to push the discomfort away. The level of discounting will depend on the amount of emotional discomfort we are experiencing in any given moment, and the patterns we have learnt over time from early childhood onwards about how to manage this type of negative affect.

6.5 Resistance

'Change is inevitable: so is resistance to change' (Moorhead and Griffin 1998, p.555). It is impossible for those implementing change to not encounter some form of resistance, discounting, reluctance or denial. Egan (1998) distinguishes between reluctance and resistance as falling into active and passive forms of avoidance. Reluctance is a passive form of avoidance (perhaps the outward sign of denial) where the person is ambiguous about the change, as they know it comes at a price. Resistance is active, when people feel forced into a situation of changing or doing something they don't want to. It can come from the organisation, the individual or both. We are all very familiar with the usual responses such as 'we haven't got the time for this relationship stuff' or 'just let me get on with my job – I'm here to teach'. In some schools, disaffected, resistant staff will ooze negativity and recruit amongst parents' groups with complaints about standards dropping. As change agents, we have some control over the level of individual resistance by using processes that encourage buy-in and engage staff in ways that reduce the levels of anxiety and fear (see Blood and Thorsborne 2005; Blood 2005; Morrison, Blood and Thorsborne 2005). Interestingly enough, the more we embrace restorative practice at a whole school level, the less we should encounter resistance as we involve and work with others in these intensely relational ways.

Change, by its nature, involves stepping into the unknown and taking risks. This takes courage. For the majority who are risk-adverse, this will be too confronting. Some will be able to comprehend this information and sit with the uncertainty. The vast majority (94%) will want to deny the need for change, or deny the seriousness of the problem for a multitude of reasons that make good sense to them, or they will sit and wait and see.

Chapter 7

Elements of an Effective Change Process

So far we have considered how people cope with change, how change is an emotional process, why change fails, the nature of resistance and denial. We have examined how all of these considerations need to be managed if the implementation of restorative practice is to be successful. Now we consider the elements of effective implementation.

In our experience, most schools embark on the implementation of restorative practice without being aware of what effective implementation looks like and without awareness of the complexities of change management. The exceptions to the rule are those who have taken time to investigate the implementation as change management and from the start look to build sustainable practice. Sadly, often, staff are tasked with attending a workshop on RP, with their job to 'cascade' the skills to the whole school on their return. When we meet them some time later, we inevitably hear heartbreaking tales of how difficult the process has been. In reality, would we send the star player of a team off to coaching school, to then come back and train the whole team? If we were playing park football, then yes we might do that, but in reality we would not expect a player in a serious team to do that. Yet, time and time again, schools and workplaces try to cut corners by expecting the same of their staff. Rather than saving funds, the schools then end up losing time and having to start again from scratch, whilst even more sceptical staff watch on, having seen what happened the first time around.

This book is designed to assist schools, and implementation teams in particular, to be very clear about what they are intending and how they are going to make this happen, getting it right the first time, rather than having to learn through trial and error. If incremental change is what is required, then it is about being conscious of how long this process will take to achieve the desired effects, and knowing it will not happen overnight.

7.1 First and Second Order Change

Let's look firstly at the environmental factors to determine whether you are embarking on first order or second order change as you consider the implementation of restorative practice. This may help you determine how you use this resource and whether you might need to rethink the implementation of restorative practice to better align with the type of change that you are considering.

First order change is about tinkering with what you already have. This type of change is incremental and often the result of:

- not understanding the need to align practice and vision (a common problem)

- not being willing to challenge and forgo old paradigms

- the barriers being too great for second order change

- wanting to trial practice on a small scale (although this might be part of an initial step to engage in second order change), or

- the school environment and culture already being conducive to the implementation of restorative practice in that it is already deeply relational and focused on wellbeing. The changes needed are less tectonic!

Some of the reasons for opting for first order change include:

- the lack of a mandate for whole school change

- insufficient resources – both financial and at a staffing level

- new leadership team wanting to find their way

- there is an urgent need to do something to address behavioural issues

- choosing to trial the efficacy of practice, before rolling out across the school

- not yet sure about the practice

- there is a conversation that there is 'nothing wrong around here' or 'no need to change'
- people are comfortable with the status quo
- challenging culture amongst staff or difficult, powerful factions
- simply do not have the capacity for whole school change, or
- restorative practice has been seen as just another 'tool' in the behaviour management tool bag.

If real long-term sustained culture change is what you want then, according to the National Academy of Academic Leadership (n.d.), *second order change* is what is really needed. We agree with this notion. The school actually has to do something significantly or fundamentally different from what is presently happening. The process is deemed irreversible, as once begun it is difficult to return to the way things were. This level of deep change is not for the faint-hearted.

Let us provide some examples of schools that have embarked on first and second order change. As we do so, it is important to understand that first order change may be completely appropriate or be the only option available in your school in the beginning. It is important to understand the rationale for why you have selected each option and to know what is possible.

It is our view that first order change around the implementation of restorative practice is only successful in building sustainable practice when the environment is conducive to change. This requires a strong relational focus that is values-driven and the implementation of restorative practice is aligned with a school vision that is relational in nature.

Case Study A: Unconscious First Order Change

There are of course many reasons for opting for first order change and School A is representative of these. Basically the school sends someone to get trained in RP – quite often someone outside of the leadership team – who is then required to train others or to implement a whole school approach to RP without the resources or the time to do so. Alternatively, the school hires a consultant to do a whole school introductory day, believing that staff are now trained and there is nothing further needed. Within 6–12 months the conversation invariably turns to 'We tried that and it didn't work' or 'We just cannot get staff to buy into this'. In turn, the staff member tasked with implementation burns out or moves on from that role, or the school. In this case, the leadership has underestimated what it takes to implement restorative practice in a school that has not been readied for change. The same applies to the implementation of any change initiative in a school. Whilst there are some ideas that are easier to implement than others, by and large most change initiatives fail, as we have discussed earlier. First order change can work, though, as in the case of the next example.

Case Study B: Conscious First Order Change

School B was a small community school with a strong community presence and vision. The school community was clear that generally things worked well in their school and there were few issues that concerned them. Students were generally well-behaved and largely compliant in their behaviour, although a new principal coming from a restorative school could see the potential to do things better, to build stronger relationships and to encourage the students to take more responsibility for their actions. The school leader's view was that the teachers were doing too much of the regulating in the classroom and whilst the school did not have many problems, the potential was there for this to change. As a result, the leader talked to the staff about building on their gains and tweaking what they did. All staff were then introduced to informal RP practice and preventative Circle Time. A large part of the focus was developing a consistent language across the school community and sharing this with students and parents alike. In this case, the school did not need second order change; rather, it needed to tweak what was already working. An interesting aspect of the time spent with this school is that there was an outward façade that, when tested, was found to be a little unstable underneath. It is once again a reminder of how even the slightest change can still cause ripples that impact people in different ways. Because the change was conscious, the school leader worked with this and used the opportunity to talk about how they as a group could build resilience and continue to improve their school.

Case Study C: Second Order Change

School C was a small primary Australian school located in a capital city, primarily drawing on a low socio-economic population of families and students. Many parents were struggling, some were in prison, some in state housing or suffering mental health and addiction issues. The school had a poor reputation and essentially no one, including staff, wanted to be there. Students only attended as a result of having no other options and attendance was sporadic. Parents would not walk in the school door and if they did, they would often be rude and abusive to staff.

The new school principal embarked on second order change, as the imperative was so great. Not to do so would have risked a declining school population with poor academic results, and the possibility of closure. There was no turning back. Initially, the school leader focused on developing an approach using the FISH[11] philosophy and developed a new school vision. His approach was completely relational, each morning walking the school, meeting and greeting parents at the front door, visiting classrooms and building relationships. He then organised training to complement the school vision and ensured that he and his staff were appropriately skilled. They adopted strategies with the complete vision of enhancing outcomes for every school student. They did not have an implementation team. Instead the school was small enough to bring everyone on board. It was clear that all owned the process and practice was embedded well.

By the time the school leader finished his tenure some five years later, he left a school that was a model RP school where many an 'intending RP' school had visited. Parents came into the school each afternoon and openly interacted with staff and teachers, teachers wanted to be there, school enrolments had increased dramatically and academic outcomes were greatly enhanced. Students were engaged and wanted to be there. It was a school that lived and breathed the RP and FISH philosophy. It was relational and highly restorative in nature, to the point that one young boy asked the principal for a conference one day, only for the principal to establish in the process that the boy was the main perpetrator. At the end of the process, the principal asked why he had requested a conference, to which the student said, 'It was really easy. I did the wrong thing, felt bad and knew you would help me to fix it up' (P. Ross, personal communication 2009).

There are many schools that have embarked on second order change, always with the end in mind and a clear understanding of what it is that they are about to embark on. Invariably they make resources available, are on the search for or have received funding to support professional development, are willing to do what it takes, and have the leadership driving the change initiative. Thankfully, there are an

---

1   FISH is a workplace management system created by John Christensen that focuses on developing a positive climate for workers and customers.

increasing number of these schools throughout the world, as schools learn from one another and the resources become available to help inform this practice.

7.2 The Elements of Effective Change

Effective implementation of RP and therefore cultural change, whether that be first or second order change, requires vision, skills, incentives, resources and an action plan in order to operationalise the change initiative and to achieve the vision. Figure 7.1 is an adaptation from Knoster, Villa and Thousand (2000) that outlines the elements of an effective change process. This includes vision, skills, incentives for change, resources to make it happen and an action plan.

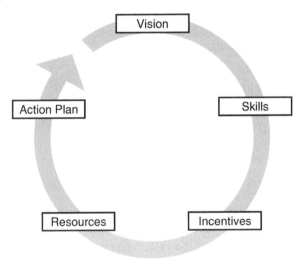

Figure 7.1 Elements of effective change processes (adapted from Knoster, Villa and Thousand 2000)

The absence of any of the five elements will have a direct impact on how people respond to the change. For example, the absence of a clear vision that is shared and understood by all staff will lead to a state of *confusion*. Without a sense of the big picture, there will be a lack of direction. If those who are required to implement or to change their way of doing things do not have the required *skills*, then change will be thwarted, as in the case of the school that opts for a one-day introductory session or short course training and do not follow up with additional skills development or an ongoing dialogue with staff. Some people will be naturals at this work, whilst others will need to observe and wait for the methods to be tested, before they will be willing to give this a go. Repeat practice sessions will allow for refinement and bringing staff on board. Without this, anxiety will increase, as will the conversation that *we tried that and it didn't work*.

People also need some form of an *incentive* in order to adopt new practice in terms of what's in it for them. This is a theme that has been echoed throughout the research. Unless staff know how it will make their life easier or how this connects with everything else they do, they will resist efforts to implement. We have talked about the links between RP and pedagogy earlier in this book. Change has to make sense and not be change for the sake of change. Change without *resources* can only lead to frustration. It is somewhat akin to baking a cake without the key ingredients – it's not going to turn out the way you had hoped it would. As Hopkins (2009) has identified, the key resources for the effective implementation of restorative practices include:

- people
- time, and
- financial resources.

In all of the examples of sustainable school practice, there have been common elements. These include the fact that school leaders identified the right people to take responsibility for the roll-out and carriage of practice; they allocated time for them to do this work and to attend ongoing professional development; and they found the funds, whether through applying for funding or allocating internal resources. We cannot think of a successful model where this has not happened.

Finally, the lack of an *action plan* will lead to many false starts or a hit and miss approach, according to Knoster *et al.* (2000). The primary aim of this book is to bring together information about effective change management processes as they apply to the implementation of restorative practice, to prevent some of these false starts from occurring.

7.3 The Rate of Adoption

The rate of change is affected by the rate of adoption of the innovation or uptake by the members of an organisation. Rogers (2003) outlines five variables that affect the rate of adoption: perceived attributes of the innovation; the social system; how the decision was made; change agent activity; and communication about the innovation. This highlights many of the variables within the implementation of restorative practice, previously referred to in our earlier papers (Blood and Thorsborne 2005; Blood 2005; Morrison *et al.* 2005). We will refer to two critical components of this model: perceived attributes of an innovation, and change agent activity.

Perceived attributes of an innovation

It will be difficult to implement an innovation if it does not make sense to those required to implement it; it does not align with core business; it is difficult or problematic to put into practice; it does not allow experimentation; and where the results are not relatively immediate and observable to the majority. Rogers (2003) details the elements of an innovation that will determine the adoption of a new idea:

1. *Relative advantage.* The innovation needs to be better or more effective than what already exists. The implementation of restorative practice has relative advantage in this regard when you compare suspension rates and the impact that this has (or hasn't had!) on student behaviour.

2. *Compatibility* (with existing values and practices). How compatible is the innovation with existing values, the needs of the potential adopters and their past experiences? What we notice in schools is that those that have values that closely align with the restorative values and those values are explicitly expressed in daily behaviours are the schools that have less resistance to RP.

3. *Simplicity* (ease of use). How difficult an innovation is to understand and put into practice affects the rate of adoption. Whilst the concept of restorative practice might be easy to

grasp by some members of staff, they nonetheless need to experiment with the practice to find out how it works and whether or not it is effective. One-off introductory sessions are not likely to assist the majority to take up practice. In fact, only those who can see how it aligns with their existing practice will do this.

4. *Trial ability.* Trial ability refers to the degree to which experimentation can occur. Successful implementation of restorative practices involves starting with a small section of the school that has the opportunity to experiment, to establish what works and what doesn't work and develop best practice – the reinvention process that is so necessary to align theory with practice. For example, some secondary schools have adopted restorative practice in their entry year as their trial, because, aside from the obvious advantages, their feeder primary schools have adopted restorative practice. It makes good sense that students are exposed to familiar processes at a difficult time of adjustment for them.

5. *Observable results.* Finally, the benefits of the implementation must be clearly observable to others. This is where restorative practice excels, as one will be easily won over when they see and experience the change in behaviour and attitude through one of the many RP processes. Sharing the stories and the impact restorative practice has had on data is vital throughout implementation. Without this, the new practice is likely to remain a mystery to others. Personal stories paint a powerful image for others. For example, a teacher, student and mother sharing their personal experiences at a large forum of teachers, students, parents and community about the impact of being involved in a restorative process was very powerful. Visual images that facilitate the sharing of these stories can also be very powerful.

Change agent activity and functions

A change agent is someone who has the capacity to influence people and innovation. The best change agents are those located within the system, but external to the school that you are trying to change. They may be a resource person who has the capacity to move in and out of the environment you are working with. It is important that they have enough distance from the workplace that they can observe from the balcony – or take an overall view – and that they develop good relationships with the practitioners on the ground.

Clarke (1999) states that change agents:

- develop the need for change

- establish a two-way information exchange

- diagnose client problems

- create the intent to change in the client

- translate this intention into action

- stabilise adoption and prevent discontinuance, and

- shift the client from reliance on the change agent to self-reliance.

Regional/county/district support staff, behaviour and educational consultants and school psychologists are often well placed to take up the role of the change agent, provided they have a helpful role with the school and the opportunity to spend time on the ground having formal and informal discussions with people. External consultants need to look for these people and to nurture their ability by coaching and mentoring them early on. In time, they will take over the role of the external consultant. It is worthwhile remembering that you too are an agent for change!

Chapter 8

The Importance of Leadership

We have grappled with whether or not to include a chapter on leadership in this book and then what to leave in and what to leave out when such a significant body of work already exists. In the end, we felt that the influence and impact of leadership on change management and sustainable implementation of restorative practice was so important, we simply couldn't leave this out. Since *relationship* has such a vital place in the restorative philosophy we also felt the need to make the connection between relationship and leadership. There is no getting away from the fact that poor leadership affects relationships and strong leadership is critical in all successful change initiatives.

Organisational change expert and writer Margaret Wheatley (1999) suggests that we can't escape from the notion of relationship. Wheatley's (2005) *Finding Our Way: Leadership for an Uncertain Time* states that there is 'an inherent organizational intelligence...present in both people and the systems that form around people' (as cited in Ghalambor 2011, p.13). Everything comes down to the relationships and how people and systems relate, as Wheatley (1999) articulates:

> Wherever you look in the natural world, you find only networks, not org charts. These networks are always incredibly messy, dense, tangled, and extraordinarily effective at creating greater sustainability for all who participate in them. All living systems are webs of relations spun into existence as individuals realize that there is more benefit available to them if they create relationships than if they stay locked in narrow boundaries of self-interest. Unending processes of collaboration and symbiosis characterize life. These relationships of mutual benefit lead to the creation

of systems that are more supportive and protective of individuals than if they had tried to live alone. It's important to remember that nothing living lives alone. (para. 8)

8.1 Leading the Way

'The most significant determinant of your organisation's culture will be the leadership style of managers at all levels' (Lee 2004, p.39). In our experience, successful implementation is heavily dependent on the quality and passion of the leadership in general within the school. Ignoring this will risk the rapid addition of any initiatives to the 'been there, done that – didn't work' list. However, the authors acknowledge that leadership can be found at many levels within the school community and therefore is not so heavily dependent on one person. Sometimes it takes the enthusiasm of a few to build a critical mass of advocates that can move things along.

8.2 Leadership Behaviours

What are the leadership behaviours that will influence, unite and inspire the school community to adopt a paradigm that for some will be a serious challenge to their beliefs and values? As Kotter (2012b) suggests: 'when an entire team of senior management starts behaving differently and embodies the change they want to see, it sends a powerful message to the entire organization. These actions increase motivation, inspire confidence and decrease cynicism' (para. 6).

Here's what, after working with schools for many years to implement a whole school approach to RP, we know for sure:

1. Schools whose senior leadership team has done intensive training to understand the whole continuum of restorative practice and the philosophy progress further than schools where they have not.

2. Those tasked with implementation must have strong and visible Senior Leadership Team (SLT) support and guidance. If there is the merest whisper of ambivalence about RP from the senior team, implementation will suffer and possibly stall.

3. Even if leaders have done the training it does not guarantee that a school will be successful in the implementation for sustainability, particularly if their *behaviours* are at odds with the RP philosophy and practice.

4. The school leadership has to have an understanding of, and support for, what is involved in organisational change.

An example of poor leadership is all too frequently seen when the Head of School and SLT are absent from the training for whole staff. Even if the team are well versed in RP, it is critical that they are seen to be present and actively engaged in the process. To not do so sends a powerful message to staff that this is not a priority and is perhaps: 'Do what I say, not what I do.' Between us, we cannot think of one school that has been successful in sustaining practice where the SLT has not been active and present in every step of the process. We can, however, cite all too many that have failed, where the boss failed to turn up on the day or was in and more often out of the process, pleading more urgent demands on their time. Of course, there are many variations to this, although the common elements of failure for schools to adopt a restorative approach start with the failure of the leadership to own, resource, support and guide the process.

This lack of support will become evident when there are decisions to be made about serious incidents of harm and how they are to be dealt with, and structural changes and approaches and consequent resourcing that are needed.

It is a no-brainer that the SLT needs to *lead* the implementation, or rather provide leadership and guidance for the change process and the team doing the hard work. We strongly suggest that a member of the SLT needs to be a part of the implementation team. This will be explored in some depth in the next section of this book. This level of clout will be necessary for decision-making and to be the public face of the change process. This person will also have to bring the rest of the leadership team along – managing across and upwards!

These leadership qualities are as important for pioneers (Early Adopters) of restorative practice in schools as they are for the school leadership. They too must engage the school community (or at least those within their sphere of influence) in useful dialogue about behaviour management in general and the restorative philosophy in particular. This means that they might have to manage upwards and may need to be taught/coached/mentored how to do this effectively.

These behaviours, happily, fit with those mentioned in John Kotter's (2012a) Eight Steps to Organisational Change, and we will be discussing Kotter's work in greater detail in the next section of this book. To illustrate these practices and to unpack the behaviours that support practice, we have created a table based on Kouzes and Posner (1997) and our own work.

Table 8.1 Leadership behaviours for change (adapted from Kouzes and Posner 2007)

Exemplary practice	Behaviour
1. Challenging the process	• Challenging the status quo; trying new approaches, innovating, taking some risks • Asking 'what can we learn?' Seeing failures and mistakes as disappointment and a learning opportunity • Setting goals, plans, milestones • Searching *outside* the school for new ways to improve *Schools that succeed in implementing RP look beyond themselves, reach out, share practice with other schools and bring new ideas back to the system.*
2. Inspiring a shared vision	• Describing a compelling and eloquent image of the future that ties into people's dreams and interests – enlisting people in this vision • Talking about future trends that will impact on education and relationships • Speaking with conviction about the meaning of our work • Linking RP into the bigger picture of education of young people *These schools have visual cues and prompts about the importance of RP, how it aligns with everything they do and it is constantly in the language – both written and spoken. It is what we do around here!*

cont.

Exemplary practice	Behaviour
3. Enabling others to act	• Fostering teamwork and collaboration; use 'we' instead of 'I' • Supporting decisions others make; giving them choices about how to do the work (sharing power and delegation) • Treating others with dignity and respect • Developing leadership in others; ensuring people grow in their jobs *Enabling, resourcing and supporting others to act will develop leadership potential across the school community in a multitude of ways.*
4. Modelling the way	• Demonstrating commitment to RP by modelling the behaviours they want to see from staff, students and parents – setting a personal example • Following through on promises and commitments • Clarifying for others his/her own personal philosophy of leadership • Building consensus around the school values so they are owned by everyone • Asking for feedback about his/her actions and its impact on others' performance (modelling being held accountable) *Actions speak way louder than words. Walking the talk, being accountable for our practice and empowering others to call us to account when this is not the case is one of the greatest gifts we can give our school community.*
5. Encouraging the heart	• Keeping hope and commitment alive by recognising efforts and contributions people make • Expressing confidence in people's abilities • Noticing commitments to shared values and making comment • Celebrating accomplishments

	It takes something special to implement and maintain practice, and you must recognise how far those who have bought in have contributed and the risk they have taken. Acknowledge their contribution and let them know you appreciate their effort. Send them to another school, forum or event to share practice and to be inspired by others. Your school will reap the benefit of this.

These behaviours cannot, we believe, be separated out from each other like an egg yolk from egg white. It's the total package that creates a recipe that is likely to do what effective leadership does – *influence others to change.* These are behaviours that must be practised 24/7; and while we are on the topic of change, if we look closely at the list in Table 8.1, these are the same sorts of behaviours that we would see in a classroom from a competent, effective, relational teacher. As the earlier quote from Meg Wheatley (1999) states: 'these relationships of mutual benefit lead to the creation of systems that are more supportive and protective of individuals than if they had tried to live (*or function*) alone' (para. 8). Nothing meaningful happens without this, which means that the 'below the green line' (see Section 3) is attended to, that people's emotional needs are met and we all feel part of something greater than ourselves – that we can make a difference to the lives of others and the way we do our work. In the final section of this book we look at what you need to do to successfully implement RP in your educational setting.

Leaders need to:

- walk the talk – be congruent

- surface the concerns

- have a good understanding of restorative practice

- align policy and practice

- deal with adult issues within the school.

Developing sustainable practice starts with the leadership team walking the talk. You simply cannot expect others to change if you are unwilling to change yourself or to align practice within the school with the restorative practice framework. If relationships are central to everything you do, then you need to model that.

Case Study: The Relational Leader

Take for example a leader of a highly successful primary school. Within 18 months, this school had gone from a place where no one wanted to work or send their children to a bustling restorative community. Any visitor to this school was bound to experience this the moment they walked in the door. It started with a warm greeting at the front door by office staff who would quickly make a few calls to track down the principal. He was notoriously challenging to find in the mornings, because he was walking the talk. You would invariably find him in a classroom talking with students and teachers, saying hello to students who would affectionately greet him in his travels. He could check in with staff to see how they were going, students were used to him in the classroom and knew he was someone that they could go to if they had a concern. If he bumped into a challenge, he dealt with it then and there and he involved affected staff in the process. He was relational and congruent in everything he did.

As Hopkins (2004) indicates, leaders who are congruent will take opportunities to have the formal and informal conversations with students, educators, parents and others within the school community. They have the more challenging conversations when they need to and they tackle the issues in a restorative and relational way. Meetings are structured to get the best from people, to involve them and to engage them in processes. Action taken is communicated with those that need to know and throughout the school as required. Most importantly, leaders in a restorative context help educators to make sense of why we are doing what we are doing in terms of how it relates to teaching and learning – the core business of education.

Blanchard (2006) suggests that leaders can help the enormity of the change process by developing strategies to bring the concerns within the organisation to the surface. People and groups will have individual concerns about the change process, dependent on how they are affected by it. This means putting aside your own busy-ness around managing competing demands to pay attention to the process, to give people a voice and to create opportunities to hear concerns and ideas.

Case Study: Leading the Way

A fine example of this was a school leader, who at time of writing is now in his third school as a principal. On each occasion he has quietly worked at developing the capacity of his staff, working out those that make a difference, those that need encouragement and support and those that need to be held to account. At the right time, he has introduced a range of initiatives, including restorative practice. He is clear on how everything is aligned, how this is a priority for the school and, importantly, how this can make a difference to their core business. Whilst leading the way, he encourages those that adopt the change also to lead the way. He resources the initiatives and he develops confident leaders, many of whom have gone on to higher positions in other schools.

He, and many others like him, have built a culture one brick at a time. As Kotter (2012a) states: 'culture changes only after you have successfully altered people's actions, after the new behaviour produces some group benefit for a period of time, and after people see the connection between the new actions and the performance improvement' (pp.164–165).

Understanding the nature of change and why change fails is critical to understanding how to effect successful change. As we have discussed in detail, change is an emotional process that requires change agents and the leadership team of a school to engage both hearts and minds in the process of effecting change. This requires a focus on tasks that are both rational (heads), and emotional (hearts). Whilst change is clearly a complex and challenging process, no matter what the nature of this change, effective leadership and people management skills will assist in this process. Given that relationships are at the core of everything restorative, it is crucial that we understand how to bring people on board.

Now that we know the critical considerations, the next section of this book provides the 'how to' of restorative practice implementation.

Making It Happen
An Implementation Guide

Chapter 9

Overview

While we have devoted the previous section of this book to understanding change and how it can affect people (excite some, send others running for cover), we would like to offer in this section of the book two basic things: a model for thinking about everything that has to be taken care of in the complex job of changing the school culture through the vehicle of RP; and step-by-step guidance to keep you grounded in that model.

In Section 2, a quote from Meg Wheatley speaks of how connected and interconnected we are with each other. We would like to add to that by reminding you of something we sometimes forget. We are after all, warm-blooded animals – mammals – biologically *social* animals dependent on these interconnections and networks for our very survival. We live in a community and we have a strong need to belong. Change done poorly will disrupt that, and in Section 2 you will have read how that can turn out for you!

9.1 Seven Circles

Understanding the change process in a school striving to become restorative is possibly best captured, we believe, by the now famous 'Six Circle' diagram (see Figure 9.1). Initially developed by Margaret Wheatley and then later developed in a collaborative effort between change management specialists such as Dalmau, Knowles, Zuieback, Staal, Capra, Rogers and others (Zuieback 2000). We have adapted the diagram from the original by adding a seventh circle that signifies the need for an inspiring vision supported by strong and deeply rooted values that interconnects the areas on both sides of the green line.[1]

Above the Line: What has to be done – System Infrastructure

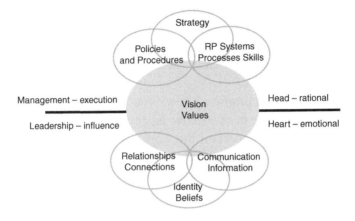

Below the Line: How it has to be done – Human Infrastructure

Figure 9.1 Seven circle diagram – Above and below
the green line (adapted from Zuieback 2000a)

Dalmau (2000) indicates that work done above the green line alone will not effect desired culture or behaviour change *because it does not tackle matters of the human heart.* In this section of our book we have confined our thinking to the work involved with implementing restorative practice, and acknowledge that this framework could be equally applied to any large-scale organisational change in the school or smaller changes within faculties.

Our understanding of this framework rests on the notion that organisational change is a matter for both heads and hearts. In work

---

1   The 'green' line was a line first drawn on butcher's paper at a workshop in green felt-tip pen by Tim Dalmau, an Australian consultant, in 1993, that separates 'systems' infrastructure from 'human' infrastructure in the original Six Circle diagram, and has since been used to reference work done 'above and below' the green line in the Six Circle diagram. We have not used green pen in our figure in this book, so *our* green line is actually black. We need you to imagine a green line!

that we have been privileged to do with First Nations people in Canada and New Zealand, one of the lessons *they* taught *us* about the restorative process was that it is as much about heart talk as it is about head talk. We see the parallels here. People in our schools will not be moved by intellectual argument alone and sorting out the rational parts above the green line, that is, putting new structures and policies in place. It all comes back to what happens *below* the green line – engaging the very people that need to buy-in and to deliver frontline services in classrooms, corridors, playgrounds and offices and that means all of us.

Experienced practitioners know how powerful the emotional transformation can be in an effective process. So, then, it is important to understand how important the work will be that is done *under the green line* where the leadership's capacity to influence people's hearts is where real change happens. The work of leadership and implementation teams has to be done above and below that green line.

The temptation for implementation teams is to spend most attention on getting the strategy, structures, operations and processes right – involving budgets and plans and policies – the work done 'above the green line', and the responsibility of effective management. This is about system infrastructure, that must be done and executed well, but it is only the rational part of change.

However, this work alone will not change the culture of behaviours in the school. What will make the most difference will be the leadership's capacity to capture the *hearts* of its staff, parents, students and governing body to influence their thinking and ultimately their behaviour. We are talking of course about *influence*. And this is what creates followership. This is the relationship work, developing connections between people and between faculties and programmes, and between the school and the community, through the development of trust – growing it, maintaining it, repairing it.

> Relationships has a far more expansive meaning than is generally thought. It has to do with how a team or organization values its people – their emotional, physical and spiritual well-being; the level of connectivity among people across the system; the value placed upon

collaboration and high functioning teams; and the level of connectivity of and the type of relationship between key teams, programs and operational systems. It is not just the traditional understanding about a focus on people getting along and liking each other. (Zuieback 2012b)

It will be about information, about two-way communication, and about understanding that 'information is like oxygen' (Zuieback 2012a, p.3). As we have discussed in the preceding chapters on why change fails and the elements of effective change processes, people have a strong need to know what's happening, why it's happening and how they might be affected. They need input and to be part of co-constructing the strategy, structures, processes and policies (above the green line) in meaningful ways (below the green line) so that this develops buy-in and creates ownership and a sense of belonging. It is doing this work *with* and *through* the people in order to bring about change in the system itself (T. Dalmau, personal communication 2013).

Lastly, or perhaps in the first instance, leaders must help their organisation to reflect on and to develop a strong sense of identity of who they are and who they want to be, captured in the vision, mission and values. What do they believe about human nature? What do they believe about the most effective way to raise a child to become loving, caring, responsible, compassionate? What are the influences in their own lives that have led them to believe what they do, and is that possible to change?

This is complex work, both above and below the green line. This attention to staff development takes serious commitment to resourcing, in terms of time and finances, and one has to be in it for the long haul. But if there is true commitment to the vision and its underpinning values, then the governing body and the leadership team will find ways to resource this development.

The implications are, then, that the school leadership and the implementation team 'gets' that this is the work that will have to be done. Not just the 'what' but the 'how'.

Chan *et al.* (2003) suggest there are four hurdles to overcome in the organisational change process: the *cognitive hurdle* that blinds employees from seeing that radical change is necessary; the *resource hurdle* that is endemic nearly everywhere; the *motivational hurdle* that discourages and demoralises staff; and the *political hurdle* of internal and external resistance to change.

In order to overcome the *cognitive* hurdle you need to make a compelling case for change by making key people come to terms with the problems within the organisation. This may include involving them in the collection of data or sharing this data which points to the overwhelming need for change. They could be involved in research which points to the ineffectiveness of current practice. Effective *resource management* may require a concentration of resources and efforts in areas most in need of change in the most efficient way. For example, if most bullying and disruption occurs in the playground, why do we only have one teacher on duty? To jump the *motivational* hurdle people must recognise what needs to be done and yearn to do it themselves. Don't try to motivate and reform the whole organisation at once, instead motivate the key influencers and those persuasive people with multiple connections, as we have referred to in Rogers' work. The *political* hurdle is addressed by identifying and silencing key opposition, with evidence that RP works. It is important to understand that when you identify key members of staff who have the ability to sway opinion then you seek to keep them on side and utilise this political influence.

In this section, and finally, we become more specific about what steps are needed for this deeper, long-term organisational change that comes from shifting hearts and minds to a place where retreat is unlikely. Staff in schools who are interested in culture change ask us: 'Where do we start? How do we move people along? What do we do about people who are going to resist? What if our senior leadership team won't support us? How will we find the time? How long will it take? How will we get our parents on board?' These are all valid questions that have been already been explored in Section 2. If there is a careful strategy that follows some well-researched pathways for organisational change, and there is a committed and powerful team driving our strategy, we are more likely to reach that place where old habits have died and been replaced by new systems, processes and, more importantly, behaviours. When these new behaviours have become the norm, then the culture has been transformed. This is not quick work, though, and as you will read, the transformation doesn't happen at the *start*. It happens at the *end*!

9.2 Eight Steps for Change

We have based our model of bite-sized steps, in the main, on the work of John Kotter (1995, 2007, 2011, 2012a,b; Kotter and Cohen 2002). We consider him to have developed the most useful framework for understanding what's needed for planning, implementing and sustaining desired change. He states that change is a 'process rather than an event' (Kotter 2007, p.1) and has developed eight key steps that we outline in Figure 9.2. We have also included a planning template (Appendix 1: Eight Step Planning Grid) that we strongly encourage your implementation team to use when engaged in actual planning activities.

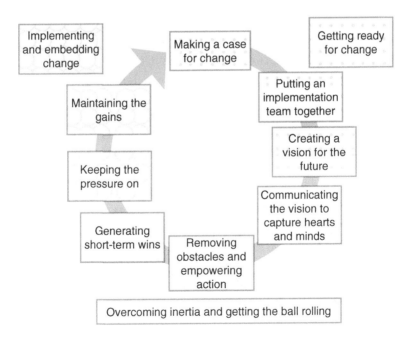

Figure 9.2 Steps for transformational change (adapted from Kotter 1995)

Kotter's (1995) steps, usually represented in a linear fashion, but shown in our diagram in a circle, are bundled into three broad stages: Getting ready for change; Overcoming inertia and getting the ball rolling; and Implementing and embedding change. Each stage has a discrete number of steps, totalling eight, which we break down in the following chapters into possible tasks, and these are as explicit as possible. Many of the practical ideas we have included have come from being directly involved in and being able to observe organisational change being managed effectively within and across a range of educational settings. Our ideas are not exhaustive and we expect that schools will find creative ways to achieve the steps in each stage.

We also believe that the change process can become quite messy and it will feel sometimes as if there have been three steps forward and two steps back. Keep in mind the need to accomplish all major steps, and even if you need to go back a bit to complete or cover a step missed, the eight steps will, in themselves, provide a useful audit checklist and are worthy of your complete attention. Kotter (1995) has numerous case studies that demonstrate quite clearly where a change process in an organisation has been held up or failed completely because an early step has not been thoroughly completed, or has been skipped entirely.

Some wise person (anonymous) once commented that the change process was like moving a load around in a wheelbarrow. The wheelbarrow only does its work when we are lifting its handles and pushing. As soon as we put the handles down and take the pressure off, movement ceases. This, too, is the case with organisational change and is why we have represented Kotter's (1995) steps in a circle. There is a need for constant renewal, to keep the practice we want to see front and centre; to overcome the tendency to slip back into old habits; and to 'enculture' new staff, new students, new parents, new governing bodies and even new senior management in the preferred way of being and doing. This takes commitment to the change process, a systematic approach to planning and implementation and strong leadership.

The planning template we provide in Appendix 1 is a road map to complete Kotter's (1995) eight steps and we encourage you to use it as a tool. While much of the planning can be done in-house, it might pay to engage someone outside the school community to facilitate some of the steps outlined. To attempt to plan for all eight stages in one sitting is a recipe for a serious case of indigestion, and it may become overwhelming. As you will see as you read on, this will in any case be virtually impossible as one cannot plan so far ahead.

The following three chapters are devoted to defining and explaining the stages and steps that are so necessary for you to achieve these changes. In the next chapter, we will concentrate on the overarching theme of *creating the climate for change*. The three steps in this chapter will be particularly useful for schools at the beginning of the journey. These steps are:

1. Making a case for change

2. Putting an implementation team together, and

3. Creating a vision for the future.

Schools further along will appreciate the logical progression of these first steps to assess whether or not they have achieved or missed major sections, in which case it would be critical to do or redo some step(s).

We like the advice of Heath and Heath (2010) who suggest that 'When you are at the beginning, don't obsess about the middle, because the middle is going to look different once you get there. Just look for a strong beginning and a strong ending and get moving' (p.93). If the steps in the next chapter can be achieved thoroughly, you will be on the way to Heath and Heath's (2010) 'strong beginning'.

Chapter 10

Getting Ready for Change

The key steps covered in this chapter are:

1. Making a case for change

2. Putting an implementation team together

3. Creating a vision for the future.

The Appendix resources that will assist you to work through this are:

- Appendix 1 Eight Step Planning Grid

- Appendix 2 Readiness for Change Checklist

- Appendix 3 Audit tools: SWOT, SOAR, FFA

- Appendix 4 Sample Detention Survey

- Appendix 5 Strategic Planning Template

- Appendix 6 Key Planning Areas.

How ready is your school to take up the challenge of culture change? Is it the dream of a few innovators, or a wider cross-section of the school community? Is there new leadership? Has there been a crisis? What is the impetus for change?

To lessen the likelihood of failure at the first hurdle, this chapter will help you understand and progress through the three key steps listed above. These should, if achieved well, be a strong beginning and lay the foundations for the next steps towards sustainability. Kotter (2012a) refers to these three steps, along with a fourth you will find in the next chapter (Communicating the Vision to Capture Hearts and Minds), as the means to achieving a kind of warming up of the organisation, ready for the changes to come.

The first four steps in the transformation process help defrost a hardened status quo. If change were easy, you wouldn't need all that effort. Steps five to seven then introduce many new practices. The last step grounds the changes in the corporate culture and helps make them stick (Kotter 2012a, p.24).

Step 1 Making a Case for Change

Change experts such as Rogers (2003), Heath and Heath (2010) and Kotter (1995) suggest that the starting place for serious organisational culture change begins with *making a case for change*. They go so far as suggesting that creating a sense of urgency will be needed to increase the motivation of staff to change their behaviours. Your school may be facing a crisis with challenging behaviours, high suspension and exclusion rates, attendance issues or poor academic achievement. It may be regarded by the system you work in as verging on failing. Creating a sense of urgency then will not be a problem!

Your school might be lucky enough not to be in such an uncomfortable state, so staff might ask why should we be bothered if we don't have 'those sorts' of behaviour issues? If this is the case, then a different argument would have to be developed. What is it that the school might want for learners that embraces deeply held values, beyond academic results? It might be important to ask if the school has clarity around its values, and if those values are evident in the behaviours of students and the adults in the school community.

One of the first questions we think is important to ask is whether or not the school is in a state of *readiness*. Are all the elements that lead to an affirmative decision to start the culture change in place? This decision to make the first steps towards taking up a restorative approach can only be made intelligently if there is a case made for change; or if the suggested change makes sense to align with existing change processes.

Do not underestimate the importance of this first step. If you proceed without this decision to at least try RP for size, the most you can expect is some isolated pockets of good practice, and to be disappointed when others do not share your enthusiasm.

This decision has to be made at some stage by the Senior Leadership Team in consultation with the school's governing body, about whether or not the innovation (RP) might achieve the outcomes the school is seeking. In other words, is it worth the effort? In Section 2 of this book, we have stressed the need for gauging the readiness of the school to adopt the philosophy (see the Readiness for Change Checklist in Appendix 2). Kotter (1995) estimates that three-quarters of the SLT must support the decision to make changes for the long-term change process to be successful. In some cases, the school may have already done valuable work around its vision and values and is poised to take up the challenge of culture change and will not find it too much of a stretch. Other schools may find it worthwhile to take a couple of steps back before trying to rush in, only to meet unnecessary resistance that in the end may at worst defeat the change process, and at best make the going very tough. The key stages required in the making the case for change process are:

1. identifying key people to do some initial research

2. identifying potential threats and opportunities

3. beginning engagement with stakeholders.

(a) Identifying key people to do some initial research

(They may or may not continue with the implementation and roll-out of RP. Their primary purpose at this point is to assemble appropriate information to assist staff in making an informed decision.)

Someone has to take the lead to begin the process of putting together enough information such as current school data, current research and evaluation of similar programmes in other schools in order to present to key stakeholders. Key activities include:

- Identify the people in the school who are already interested (Early Adopters) or show an aptitude for this work. These are the people who will need to be prepared to do some audit work ahead of decision-making. Ask them if they are interested in helping. By and large, people are willing to do this foundational work, as they are looking for ways to improve the current culture. As Fullan (2011) states, people will be engaged in something 'that is personally meaningful, and which makes a contribution to others as well as to society as a whole' (p.3). These people may not necessarily be senior managers, but it would help if they are considered credible in the eyes of staff and students.

- Arrange for this group to access basic RP training so that they are equipped to do their groundwork. It is important that they know what to be looking for as they go about the task of assembling the information to make a case for change.

- If the school has already embarked on its change process, this group could think through how the change process has so far been managed and the impact of this on stakeholders and what major areas have been done well and which ones might have been neglected.

- This group can then identify policy, curriculum and other imperatives in the system that would be enhanced by a restorative approach. It is critical that RP is integrated into the core business of the school, as we have discussed in Section 1 of this book. Other considerations might include: What imperatives are driven by government policy? Which imperatives are more local, regional, cluster or individual to the school? Think about how these imperatives would integrate with RP. Schools, regions and districts that have successfully implemented RP have developed an understanding of how this aligns with everything else that they do.

The York Region District School Board (2013), Ontario, Canada, one exceptional example of this 'putting it all together' approach, has developed a 'quilt' or matrix of all the activities and initiatives at work in their schools and how they are connected and aligned in order to develop a positive climate for learning that is equitable, inclusive, caring, respectful, safe and supportive (Figure 10.1).

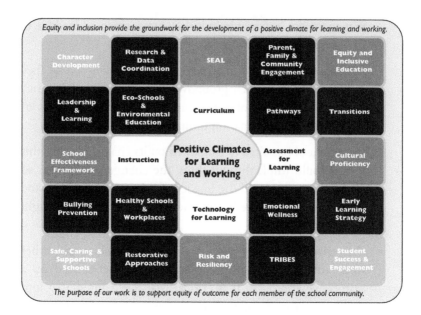

Figure 10.1 PC4L quilt: York Region District School Board:
Positive Climate for Learning and Working Strategy.[1]
Source: York Region District School Board

The Positive Climates for Learning and Working Team in the York Region District School Board, Ontario (personal communication, 2013), says of the quilt:

> We believe that collectively our work is having a positive impact in helping to clarify the message that a positive climate for learning and working is an outcome NOT another thing we have to do.

> Furthermore, we believe the philosophy behind the quilt gives all of us cause to reflect on, and articulate, how our work in both the theoretical and practical realm contributes to the development and sustainability of learning environments that are safe, respectful, equitable, inclusive, engaging and caring and how they support equity of outcome for all.

---

1   York Region District School Board, Ontario, Canada, has named RP (RA in this case) as an explicit strategy in its whole-district approach to creating a positive climate for learning and working. The quilt graphic is, in 2013, under revision, and all future related images will reflect current thinking.

Another example of an initiative, the School Wide Positive Behaviour Support (SWPBS),[2] is an approach that many schools worldwide are implementing. What are the ways in which this framework can fit with the RP philosophy? Are there areas where the philosophies don't fit? Can they be overcome? Many schools have adopted Glaser's Choice Theory[3] approach to behaviour management. Some schools have questioned the use of terms like 'behaviour' and 'management'. Some schools have adopted the use of circles to build social and emotional competence in learners. The list of programmes that are compatible with the RJ philosophy and practice are far too numerous to mention. What *is* important to understand is how everything is aligned and when it is *not* aligned, and where there is work to be done. This is likely to occur in a school that maintains a punitive approach. The old ways will eventually be challenged because they no longer fit. What imperatives would be made easier in their implementation if an RP approach were to be considered? As one school leader in a workshop in the United Kingdom once remarked, 'RP is the glue that holds everything together in our school.'

The links have to be made, otherwise staff who, too often, are overwhelmed with initiatives that aren't seen as part of a cohesive whole will sigh and say 'not another one' and batten down the hatches. As we have discussed, much change fails as a result of staff feeling overwhelmed and the resistance that this produces. Often what we assume is resistance is actually exhaustion!

- The group will have to read and provide executive summaries around best practice in the field of teaching/learning/ behaviour management. Which authors should be read? Which research will support the RP approach? What successes have

---

2   SWPBS, or School Wide Positive Behaviour Support, sometimes known by other acronyms such as PB4L (Positive Behaviour 4 Learning), is an evidence-based framework for school improvement around behaviour management. The programme assists schools to implement evidence-based approaches to managing student behaviour and related complex support issues at the local community level.

3   Glasser's Choice Theory provides one explanation for human motivation – a central aspect of Choice Theory is the belief that we are internally, not externally, motivated and that we always have choice about how to behave. It is an approach used in some schools for working with individual students to help them think about and choose more appropriate behaviours.

other schools had? Is it worth a visit to some of those schools? (See the list of recommended reading/authors to support the effectiveness of RP in the Further Reading section.)

- This research group must also engage in one key task of Kotter's, and that is to use and interrogate data. What we understand this to mean is that this is the opportunity to hold a mirror up to the school and, first, communicate some baseline data that would indicate that change is needed; second, help the school to make meaning of it (against evidence-based best practice); and third, use the opportunity to begin engaging with the wider school community. What data could be used for this step? We offer some tentative advice about the sort of data that would be useful:

  - *Qualitative data* – for example, wide dissatisfaction with the ineffectiveness of current practice evident in conversations in staffrooms and staff meetings; student and parent feedback; school reviews; union involvement in staff and student matters; positive anecdotal evidence of early forays into RP ('Wow, I tried it and it was really effective!').

  - *Quantitative data* – for example, survey data (bullying, student safety and wellbeing/mental health); exclusion and suspension/stand-down/fixed-term exclusion rates; detention rates; overuse of time-out facilities; number of students reported/sent to the office; student absences; staff absences; stress/sick leave; measures of student engagement/disengagement; academic results; retention figures.

We strongly advise, however, that building the case for the implementation of restorative practice is much more complex than relying on data that indicates that one aspect of practice, such as restorative conferencing alone, works; or relying only on data such as detention and suspension rates – these are only a small indicator of any school's culture. Data like this needs to be correlated to make good sense of it all. The exercise as a whole should be seen as an opportunity for the school to hold a mirror up and take an honest look at what it *is* doing and *claiming* to be doing. You have to start with a clear understanding of what it is that you are trying to change or improve in your school. Without a case for change, the initiative is likely to fail.

The SLT must at least be prepared to free up some time for this initial groundwork to be done. It would be a positive move for the SLT to publicly acknowledge the hard work done by these enthusiasts, so that these good people remain encouraged and engaged.

(b) Identifying potential threats and opportunities

These next steps can be used to engage a slightly wider group of school members that might include staff, parents, students and other support staff connected with the school. It will continue to contribute to engagement and support for the RP philosophy.

Two processes for analysis that we suggest are SWOT (Strengths, Weaknesses, Opportunities and Threats) or a slightly more positive, strength-based version based on Appreciative Inquiry called SOAR (Strengths, Opportunities, Aspirations, Results). You might choose to do a Force Field Analysis (FFA) instead, to identify blocking and facilitating forces. All of these are designed to provide an audit as a basis for planning and are outlined in more detail in Appendix 3. While we only mention these processes in passing at this point in this chapter, we must stress that any of these processes contributes significantly to the next stage. This would be a perfect point to engage someone outside the school community who can manage the process, while school participants provide the content.

(c) Beginning engagement with stakeholders

Change experts are clear about the need to engage stakeholders in the change process in order to gain their commitment to new ways of doing business. We are going to be asking them to make changes and, in some cases, sacrifices. It makes perfect sense to engage with the people who have to use the system, as well as the clients of that system, who, in the case of schools, are students/pupils and their parents and the wider community, although it would be fair to say that the SLT and staff are themselves 'internal' clients.

If the central value to be honoured in the school is relationships, then the way in which the school community is engaged in these early stages must reflect this value. The case for change, with all its attendant data, research and results of the SWOT, FFA or SOAR audits has to be presented to all groups of stakeholders and then a process put in place for robust dialogue and feedback. If the case is urgent, then this information will be sufficient to move at least some staff out of their comfort zones and become willing to at least consider adoption of this RP initiative.

One of the many mistakes that we have seen in schools attempting to change the school culture is the failure to maintain open communication with stakeholders. This works both ways through the sharing of information with staff, students and parents, and seeking feedback from them about the meaning of this information. Our suggestion is to use the research group to design a process for the sharing of this 'case for change' information – and then to lead the session(s) with an appropriate amount of time devoted to do this properly, rather than an agenda item in a rushed staff meeting after school. We have to *model* the value we place on engagement. It is also essential, we believe, for a member of the SLT, preferably the school leader, to introduce and conclude the session, demonstrating the support of leadership. The leadership team needs to be involved in the change process from the beginning and stay involved in a visible way throughout.

Step 2 Putting an Implementation Team Together

The key stages here are:

1. putting the team together

2. team building.

Implementing the change process is too complex and too long for it to be the work of one or two people who risk burnout; or, as is sometimes the case, someone with a strong personality who can bring people along, but when they go, so too does their influence. This work needs a team approach and in this step we pass on some valuable advice about who might be the best and most effective combination of people and skills, and perhaps more importantly, influence. And because this work is also about building relationships, we add some advice about how to build cohesion and a strong sense of purpose in the team.

(a) Putting the team together (with enough power to lead the change)

The change process needs a strong strategic approach led by people within the school who are respected and influential. Schools that are doing well with RP implementation usually have a core team/ steering group/implementation team that leads and drives the change. The renewal efforts might be led by one or two people in the beginning, but successful transformation must start with a critical mass of interested and capable people (3–5 in a small school, more in a bigger school) who will lead the change. This is also the opportunity for this group to develop its leadership capability and to encourage leadership in others.

Members need to be willing, interested and have strong positive relationships and influencing skills. In our experience, people who may be well intentioned, but have very poor social skills and poor classroom practice, would not be the best to have in the group in its early stages. Basically, the team needs to include change leaders whose power comes from a variety of sources within the school: job title, status, expertise and political influence. You will need to identify these people.

Suggested team membership includes:

- A member of the Senior Leadership Team (SLT): this person must have positional 'clout', stay committed for the long haul, and be prepared to 'model the way'. The role of the Senior Leadership Team member on the implementation team becomes critical as this person must be prepared to teach, coach and engage other members of the SLT in all of the aspects of the change process.

- An individual staff member (or several) who has a positive reputation in managing students and classroom dynamics –

and who has healthy and mutually respectful relationships with students, other staff and parents.

- A middle manager (head of syndicate, team or faculty) who has a positive influence amongst other middle managers.

- People who can design and facilitate effective and engaging internal professional development.

- Staff with specialist expertise (e.g. able to develop systems for data collection).

- A staff member other than teaching staff (e.g. teacher aide/ assistant).

- A staff member who is willing, but possibly doubtful – this person would be useful as a devil's advocate and expose flaws in plans and might fit Rogers' Early Majority and Late Majority categories, but they are still respected by other staff. It is important that this person is seen as representing the views of other staff who may not be totally sold on the idea of an RP approach. If this team member can be convinced, they will convince these others.

- Members of a committee in the school whose 'patch' fits with the RP agenda (e.g. Student Welfare Committee, Pastoral Care team, School Chaplain).

We stress again the need for a team that has influence amongst the school community as they will be leading the change process.

It might be necessary to call for expressions of interest to join the team, or invite people where you think it valuable to include a person who does not immediately put their hand up. If the numbers exceed what's needed, then some sort of process will need to be developed to choose the most effective contributors. To save the possible offence of not including someone who has offered, suggest that they will be asked to join a sub-committee to work on a particular project down the track. Once formed, your guiding coalition/implementation group will need to work as a team, continuing to build that sense of urgency and momentum.

An effective team size is around 5–8 people. Bigger than this risks people thinking someone else is always there to do the work, so it won't matter if they don't show for a meeting. Too small and we risk burnout for these dedicated people. Team members must be willing to meet on a regular basis for the duration of the implementation. At first this might mean weekly or fortnightly in the developmental phases, then maybe 2–3 times per term when the work is bedded down. Support by SLT must be given to this team to meet on a regular basis or the change is unlikely to happen.

The team will be able of course, from time to time, to co-opt others for particular tasks. Give some thought to whether a group of students might be a sounding board for suggestions and feedback. It might be worthwhile to consider using an existing student group (e.g. Student Council) for the task, or create a specific student reference group. It is imperative that students who find themselves in the referral, time-out or detention systems are canvassed about whether or not these strategies are effective in achieving the outcomes we dream they do! (See Appendix 4 for a sample student and staff detention survey.) You might even consider asking a parent who has the time available to join the task group or have interested and influential parents create their own reference group. Most certainly, working with the parent association and school board is a critical part of the process. When the time comes for appointing a new school principal or head, the governing body needs to be very clear that the change process will not be set back by the new appointment.

The team will also need to plan for succession when staff move on, or as is often the case, get promoted to other positions as a result of their developing leadership capacities. Bringing in new blood with new perspectives to the team also has its advantages with fresh eyes on the change process.

(b) Team building

Kotter (2007) suggests that a minimum level of trust must be developed in the coalition that you form to guide the implementation. Since this group exists outside the usual hierarchy of the school, it will be critical that this group develops a commitment to each other as a team, unified by the vision and the task ahead. This will be a case of needing the members of this group to connect their hearts as well as their heads.

In a restorative school where relationships are at the centre of being and doing, Kotter's (2007) advice makes perfect sense. It would be worth budgeting for an offsite retreat, facilitated again by someone external to the school community, to build a sense of purpose and community within the team. If this is done carefully, not only can the team push forward together with the planning, it can develop some values and behaviours for its own robust health and wellbeing. Members of the team must feel safe to call it if something is going astray, and to concentrate on a restorative approach to solving its own issues. It must walk the talk, and be seen to do so, whilst creating the vision and strategic plans for the implementation of RP and then engaging the wider school community. We discuss the work involved in this in Step 4.

Step 3 Creating a Vision for the Future

The key stages in creating a vision are:

1. developing a vision statement – a short summary that captures the future

2. determining the values central to the change

3. creating a strategy to launch and execute the vision

4. becoming fluent in describing the vision.

In any change process, the people required to make the changes need to know why they need to make changes and where they are going. In the previous section we looked at the 'why'. In this step we look at the 'where'. None of us are likely to embark on a journey needing us to change significant behaviours if we don't know where we are going. If the vision is missing, how will we know where we are heading? How will decisions be made? What are the values that will underpin everything we do? What will be the evidence of those values in action? The four stages we describe will help you cover the bases of this vital step.

(a) Developing a vision statement: a short summary that captures the future

This is such an important stage that we think this process of developing a vision statement ought to be facilitated by a skilled outsider so that the implementation team can be immersed *in the process* of developing the vision instead of trying to guide the process at the same time. If transformational change is sought, then the capturing of hearts and minds in the vision statement becomes a central focus of this part of the process.

The process can begin with a question; something like: 'If we were a perfect example of a school operating on an RP platform, what would the culture of the school look like, sound like, feel like in three years' time?'

There may be some other questions you ask each other in a visioning process before capturing the essence in a short statement. We have found the following questions to be helpful:

- What is the purpose of schooling – why do we exist?

- What is the *moral* purpose of schooling?

- What would the school look like, feel like, sound like in 3–5 years?

- What would relationships be like between all members of the school community? How would people be relating to and with one another?

- What would the wider community (external to the school) be saying about the school?

- What will we be known for three years down the track?

- What would student behaviour look like?

- What would staff behaviour look like?

- What would the behaviour of the SLT look like?

- What would be the nature of parent involvement?

- What would the relationship be like between the school and parents?

- What would we be doing to build relationships? How would we be managing the minor issues that arise?

- How would we be resolving staff issues?

- What evidence would there be to show the school values in action?

- What would be the evidence that we are succeeding?

- *Who are we?* (This is an important question that gets at perceptions of the identity of the school.)

- What kind of aspirations do we have?

- What's at the heart of what we do here? Indeed, it goes back to one of these first questions: 'Why do we exist?'

In other words, what's that *place* we want our students/pupils/school to get to?

The answers to all these questions need to be summarised into a succinct and envisioning statement of purpose that captures the central themes that emerge – in a couple of sentences (i.e. *vision*) that capture what you want the change to look like.[4] This could mean working with your existing school vision and values statement and supplementing it with an inclusion about RP; how RP will help the school achieve that vision/mission; and a recognition that RP is a larger organisational strategy itself which will help achieve that vision (e.g. improved results; safe learning community; responsible citizenship). Or you may just wish to adapt the present school vision statement and values if they reflect the relationship-based approach that you want to achieve. We believe strongly that a school needs to be explicit about the centrality of *relationship* in its endeavours and whatever the statement you develop, it must capture both hearts and minds.

Kotter (2012) also suggests that in order for the vision to be easily communicable it should be:

---

4   This URL contains a range of samples of vision statements from leading companies and organisations: www.samples-help.org.uk/mission-statements/sample-vision-statements.htm. The same website has instruction and advice for constructing school vision statements.

- simple (no jargon)

- vivid (a picture is worth a thousand words)

- repeatable (by anyone) and

- invitational (this suggests two-way communication).

Kotter (2012) states: 'A clear vision serves three important purposes. First, it simplifies hundreds or thousands of more detailed decisions. Second, it motivates people to take action in the right direction even if the first steps are painful. Third, it helps to coordinate the actions of different people in a remarkably fast and efficient way.'

Kotter (2012, p.74) goes on to state that effective visions have six key characteristics:

1. *Imaginable.* They convey a clear picture of what the future will look like.

2. *Desirable.* They appeal to the long-term interest of those who have a stake in the enterprise.

3. *Feasible.* They contain realistic and attainable goals.

4. *Focused.* They are clear enough to provide guidance in decision-making.

5. *Flexible.* They allow individual initiative and alternative responses in light of changing conditions.

6. *Communicable.* They are easy to communicate and can be explained quickly.

The following schools, one each from Australia and Hong Kong, are committed to restorative approaches to problem-solving. They have generously allowed us to use their vision/mission statements as examples here.

Case Study: Noosa District State High School, Australia
The Vision
Excellence Through Diversity. Noosa District State High School aims to provide a safe, harmonious environment that empowers students to excel as lifelong learners and become active, responsible citizens.

Values

Noosa District State High School is a student-centred learning community that fosters care and compassion. We aspire to be aware of others and their culture, accept diversity within a democratic society, and acknowledge and enjoy the rights and privileges of Australian citizenship.

    Be Responsible

    Be Respectful

    Be An Active Learner

Case Study: Discovery College, Hong Kong

The College's Vision Statement of *Grow Discover Dream* recognises the need for students to be independent, critical and creative thinkers, equipped with the skills, attitudes and values to contribute positively in this complex world in which we live.

    Grow: Be passionate about being the best we can be.

    Discover: Find wonder in the world around us.

    Dream: Dare to make a difference for yourself, humanity and our planet.

While the words 'restorative justice' or 'practice' are not to be found in the actual vision/mission statements themselves, once they are unpacked in conversation it becomes clear that RP is a key strategy that is used to achieve the vision. The work done to achieve these statements is often laborious, sometimes painful as differing values surface, time-consuming and never managed in one sitting! We can only imagine the time taken and the consultation that occurred to get these statements to this stage. What we like about them is how succinct they are, and how closely they seem to stick to Kotter's (2011) guidelines. They can be found on their respective school websites.

(b) Determining the values central to the change

Most schools have a list (usually 3–5) of values such as respect, excellence, tolerance, responsibility, life-long learning and so on. These values underpin the vision, and in the process of developing or adapting the vision, these have to be made explicit. We can comment here that it would be a rare school where a visitor could ask a random pupil, staff member or parent what the key values are in the school and be answered with total certainty and without hesitation. The issue here is that unless the values are *known* and explicitly understood, along with the behaviours derived from those values, it becomes difficult to have conversations about breaches of those values.

The values that underpin the vision have to be evident in action. The usual approach that schools take is to be very explicit about the behaviours that students need to demonstrate. What some schools miss is the critical importance of *modelling these values by the adults in the school community* – do as I do, rather than do as I say.

The central message here is that values are of no value unless the behaviours that exemplify the value are named and practised by all members of the school community. The more explicit the values and their behaviours, the less wriggle room! Indeed, it would then be possible to have a conversation with either a student *or* a staff member where there has been an incident or issue, intentional or otherwise, about the value that had been breached. We have found it far more helpful to have conversations about breaches of values rather than breaches of rules. One of the bitter pills that we ask staff to swallow with this change of culture is around the issue of personal and professional accountability. What's good for the goose is good for the gander! In other words, if we are using a process to hold students accountable, then we must hold each other accountable for our behaviours that breach those values we collectively decided were important. It is equally important to acknowledge adult and student behaviours that are positive examples of the values in action. We respond very positively when we are, and feel, encouraged.

One British school we know of has introduced its behaviour policy[5] with these words:

> Achieving good relationships in school depends on every member of staff understanding that adults need to model the behaviour they wish to see from students, that good behaviour needs to be taught as much as academic content and that lapses in behaviour can be a learning opportunity for students to develop their

---

5   At the time of publication, this school is still in the process of having its new policy approved through its governing body and hence it would not be fair to name the school at this point.

emotional literacy. We are a restorative school and all
staff are expected to use restorative process as a starting
point for resolving issues.

In our eyes, that is pretty explicit!

The SLT and implementation team can lead the way on this by
sharing stories of how they have changed their behaviour. None of
us are perfect and, if we are in such a leadership position, we must
model that we are prepared to be reflective about our own actions.
Who hasn't lost it in response to an annoying situation, especially
when we are tired and harried?

The following example describes how a senior manager (SM), also
on the implementation team, helped to change hearts and minds in
a deeply punitive school that had developed a vision for a different,
restorative future.

Case Study: Values into Behaviours

A student with challenging behaviours had made an embarrassing fuss
at an important assembly where there was a guest speaker. The SM
admonished this boy in front of everyone at the school assembly after the
guest had left. In response to the public dressing down, the student lost
his temper, said some inappropriate, disrespectful things and stormed
off. It would be easy to think that the student was the only one needing
to take responsibility for his behaviour as he clearly deserved the rebuke.
But in this case, the SM thought long and hard about his actions that day
and sought to lead the way, especially as he was a critical member of the
implementation team. *His* behaviour had not matched newly developed
and stated values.

The SM first went to the student and found out what was going
on for him. He started with apologising for the public dressing-down
and acknowledged how it probably had been difficult for the student to
manage in front of the whole school. The student said it had angered
him, which is why he swore and left the assembly. He apologised for
his own behaviour and the two went on to have a lengthy conversation
about what was going on for the student. This conversation uncovered
issues that the school could address with the student, his teachers and
his family. The SM repaired the relationship and put in place a way for
the student to start to manage his behaviour more effectively. Above all
else, it was made clear that the behaviour was inappropriate, that the
school had greater expectations and they would assist the student to
achieve this.

> The SM continued to think about his actions that day and asked the principal for time at the next assembly. He addressed the whole school by leading with a public apology to the student concerned, stating how humiliating that it had been for the student and how he regretted his own actions as a Senior Manager that day. He then talked about the need for respect of self and for others at all times and especially when there was a visitor to the school.

This rather simple act in a punitive culture was a wonderful example of leading the way and a demonstration of what is good for students is equally good for adults in the school community. It sent a powerful message about behaviour change.

(c) Creating a strategy to execute the vision

Creating a strategic plan for rolling out RP across the school community will be the next task for the team. Again we suggest an outside facilitator to free the team up so they can participate in the process and concentrate on dialogue. The first step to is make sure that the plan to implement RP is firmly embedded into the school's wider strategic plan. We offer Fairholme College[6] and Moama Anglican Grammar[7] as just two examples of schools where RP is named and firmly embedded into the pastoral care/discipline systems. Many schools that have embraced the RP philosophy have not explicitly named it in their school vision/mission statement, but a closer examination of policy documents might reveal threads that indicate its presence. If this is the case in your school, we recommend that you look for opportunities to include key RP initiatives in important documentation in the school when opportunities for review emerge. Without this, it will be difficult to engage the Late Majority and Laggards down the track, especially when they ask questions about new protocols and processes: 'Where does the policy say that?'

A template for creating a strategic plan is included as Appendix 5. This is only a sample of a strategic process with a time period of 1–3 years, and we encourage you to explore other formats that might suit your purposes better. The areas for planning are likely to emerge as a result of your SWOT, FFA or SOAR analysis and may be different

---

6　www.fairholme.qld.edu.au/index.php/83.

7　www.moamagrammar.nsw.edu.au/about/the_school.

from the ones we mention below. This is of course the work to be done above the green line – the system infrastructure that needs to be put in place – the 'what' (see Section 2). *How* this work is done will make the difference in capturing people's hearts as well as their heads, that is, it will make a difference in how hard you have to work to get the change you want.

Our experience around the major areas for planning would indicate that there are several key areas:

- *Systems*. Structures, protocols, procedures, flowcharts, roles and responsibilities, data capture, performance development and management.

- *Learning and Growth (L&G)*. This will need to be delivered by a combination of external and internal consultants. The cost of using only an external consultant will be impossible to sustain and eventually the team will need to be self-sufficient. Using the Early Adopters to do some of this later on will be critical to bring others on board, as they are seen as having credibility within the system, and it will help develop their leadership qualities.

- *Policy*. Do not be in a rush to re-write the school's policy around discipline/pastoral care until such time as you know what you want in it. That is, you will need to experiment before you know what you want to include. It is also important that you maintain a known structure whilst entering into major change. It is important not to throw the baby out with the bathwater! Not everything may need to be changed, but what does exist needs to be filtered through the vision and values and philosophy of RP.

- *Resourcing*. RP needs to have its own budget line in the school's Annual Plan to cover staff development and other costs involved in operational matters around RP processes. This is an investment for the long term.

It will become evident in your planning that these areas will overlap significantly. Resourcing and Learning and Growth will dovetail with new systems and structures that may be developed. More detailed information about these strategic planning areas are included in Appendix 6.

(d) Becoming fluent in describing the vision

The vision, or a version of it, needs to be communicated in such a way that is clear and compelling, and can be done in less than five minutes. We like to think of having to describe the vision to someone sitting next to you in a train or plane, or to a salesperson in a store, at immigration at international airports or at a dinner party – someone who has maybe asked out of politeness rather than genuine interest, but as result of your answer about the future is at once interested. It must hold appeal to both the mind and the heart.

What we suggest is some sort of group activity for the SLT and implementation team where smaller groups collaborate to develop short versions of the vision with its key themes, exchange ideas and settle on a couple that are easily practised on each other first, before unleashing them on the folk sitting next to us on planes, in trains, at dinner parties. We know this all too well from having to explain the work that we do to many strangers in our travels. Having a succinct and brief statement will engage them in a further conversation, rather than put them to sleep or back to their magazines, as the example below highlights. The same applies in conversations in our schools. We need to inspire others to say, 'That sounds interesting – tell me more...'

Case Study: Author Marg Thorsborne

I have, for years, been trying to perfect the ideal theme around RP for such an event. When asked what I do, I usually respond with, 'I help schools to make their discipline for learning more effective.' The usual remarks that follow include references to a longed-for past when a good clip under the ear or a good boot up the rear end or thrashing was all it took. I don't rise to that bait, but comment that punishment is one way to hold someone accountable, but another way, infinitely more powerful, is to bring the person who has done wrong face-to-face with the person they have harmed in order to talk about the harm and decide together what to do to fix the damage. In other words, it gives the victim a voice in the process.

While this is not an example of a dinner party vision statement about a school, its message is strong and captures one essence of RP in a nutshell, sufficient for the audience.

Once the essence of the vision has been captured, then comes the big effort! This involves infecting others with the interest and excitement, hope and optimism about the possibilities of an uplifting future, despite the fact that they may need to make some changes; to give up some comfortable habits in order to make gains they can only imagine at this point.

Remember, the overall purpose of these steps and the first in the next chapter is to warm people up. In the next chapter, we will take you through the steps that will help you get the ball rolling and that warm-up happening.

Chapter 11

Overcoming Inertia and Getting the Ball Rolling

The key steps covered in this chapter are:

1. Step 4 Communicating the vision to capture hearts and minds

2. Step 5 Removing obstacles and empowering action

3. Step 6 Generating short-term wins.

The Appendix resources that will assist you in working through these are:

- Appendix 1 Eight Step Planning Grid

- Appendix 6 Key Planning Areas.

When thinking about overcoming inertia, two things come to mind. First, a remembered physics lesson from long ago about the extra force needed before movement happens (think pushing a stationary car); and second, the need to infect people with a sense of interest and excitement! In other words there needs to be a determined and strategic effort invested in getting the message across about what the new future will be (extra push of the car) and at the same time the message has to be engaging, optimistic, hopeful, inspiring and enticing!

Once movement has started, the path has to be cleared, so the team needs to be given some space to experiment and the leadership needs be prepared to work with them to remove some of the obstacles that might stand in the way of achieving the vision. Because the work being done is usually so new, it is important that those watching see the success of targeted restorative strategies. These need to be communicated as good news stories and this will keep hopes up and motivation intact. The following three steps outline these in detail.

Step 4 Communicating the Vision to Capture Hearts and Minds

There is absolutely no point in having a vision for the future if it remains a secret in a school's yearly strategic or operational plan folder or is held tightly by the implementation team! How well this part of the process is done will determine the success of the next steps. While it might be perfectly appropriate for someone from the SLT, most likely the principal or head teacher, to make a one-off announcement along with some bells and whistles, the vision needs to be talked about at every available opportunity, and via every available vehicle. A simple message that might even be a couple of words – a summary of the vision – can be cleverly inserted into some of the most basic day-to-day communications. We suggest that the word 'relationship' could be built into these announcements. This whole issue is about *message management* – a vital part of communicating the vision.

The vision (or its short form) needs to be communicated through every channel possible – newsletters, staff meetings, parent evenings, school assemblies and the school website in a way that captures the imagination and triggers interest and possibly excitement, and leaves people feeling uplifted about the possibilities. Young people should be able to voice it, and so should staff. When the school is spoken about in the wider community, one might hope there could be some sort of sense of the vision in those conversations.

Kotter (2012b, p.97) reminds us that effective information transfer relies on repetition:

> A sentence here, a paragraph there, two minutes in the middle of a meeting, five minutes at the end of a conversation, three quick references in a speech – collectively, these brief mentions can add up to a massive amount of useful communication, which is generally what is needed to win over both hearts and minds.

Here are some other ways to get the message about the vision across to increase buy-in:

- Incorporate the vision for change into ongoing, daily communication and correspondence (we suggest especially that senior and middle managers thread mentions about the restorative changes, philosophy or reasons for it into all professional discussions where appropriate, including performance conversations).

- Ensure that the school website reflects the essence of the vision, even if the word 'restorative' is not used.

- Include stories, handy hints (for parents too) and small articles in the school newsletter as a regular feature.

- If the school uses social networking to communicate, find ways to insert the messages about relationships, and develop an appropriate policy for the healthy management of relationships via social networking.

- Create a brochure to explain the restorative philosophy and school policy and protocols for the enrolment process, so that parents and students have this explained up front.

- Make sure that induction processes for all people who are new to the school include more than a passing mention of RP. RP needs to be part of a 'the way we do things here' message and is hopefully reflected in all recruitment processes for staff, students and parents.

Since this whole piece about communicating the vision is about increasing buy-in and decreasing resistance (warming everybody up), then all efforts are really about *message management*. There are a couple of issues that, if done well, will certainly increase buy-in, and if done poorly will increase resistance. In particular we mean:

- Senior leadership needs to *walk the talk*. They must show with new behaviours that they mean what they say. In other words, they must lead by example. Kotter (2012) writes that 'when an entire team of senior management starts behaving differently and embodies the change they want to see, it sends a powerful message to the entire organization. These actions increase motivation, inspire confidence and decrease cynicism' (para. 7).

- The vision 'test' must be applied to all aspects of the school operations. If it fits the vision, it stays, if it doesn't, then whatever it is (structure, process, policy) will have to be changed or at least adapted – although with great care and consultation. If, for example, we are focusing on classroom management protocols, and current practice runs counter to the vision (for example, removing students from class for minor issues that could be dealt with in class) then senior leaders will need to make it clear what it is they want to see instead and follow through if it doesn't happen. They also need to provide support to assist teachers about how to do things differently. Remember that the implementation of RP takes time and not everyone will be confident in his or her practice from the beginning. Patience and support is important in terms of asking people to do things differently.

- Where decisions have to be made that do not fit the vision, these inconsistencies need to be explained in a transparent, honest way so that people do not become unnecessarily resentful and resistant, wondering if there are two sets of rules – one for us and one for them.

- Staff, students and parents who are affected by the changes will need regular, structured opportunities to raise their concerns and talk about any anxieties they may have. This willingness to listen by the SLT and the implementation team will help enormously. It is extremely important that this part of the process reflects the whole philosophy of how important relationships are, and people are given a voice. When we disagree, we need the opportunity to work through this and/ or to present a case for an alternate or adapted approach.

Step 5 Removing Obstacles and Empowering Action

Heath and Heath (2010) call this part of the change process 'Shaping the Path' (p.187) and suggest that often if the situation can be changed, behaviour will change. One of their suggestions in particular is to tweak the environment. Some implementation teams have made major decisions, for example about no longer using a Time-Out or Withdrawal Room. Some schools have changed the length of breaks, or even timetables. These are major situation-changers!

There are major considerations when arriving at this part of the change process, and the Senior Leadership Team must visibly support the efforts of the implementation team:

- People in the change team need to be given permission to take risks in developing new and different ways of working with students, parents and each other. If the senior leadership team is risk-averse, this experimentation will stall. The reformers need to be given space to develop new ways of doing things. Our advice is to let the implementation team decide what, how, where and when to try some new approach, trial it (always in draft), collect data and feedback and then continue to adapt structures and processes until they are delivering the desired outcomes.

- The whole system may need to be overhauled, but the decisions about where to start will be important. We suggest starting small but with highly visible changes that are likely to work, and that will produce visible results. Suggestions about what structures might need changing can be found in Appendix 5. A trial might be an important first step. Make sure that any trial is not a random event, but carefully thought through so that it is talked about openly, all stakeholders (including parents and students) are involved in giving feedback and suggestions for improvement, data is collected and people stay engaged in the process.

- It is vital that people who are being asked to do things differently are given the skills needed to do so. A programme of ongoing professional development that is (a) effective, (b) built on adult learning needs and (c) clearly and explicitly linked to the vision needs to be delivered. Having this change (skill acquisition and practice) linked then to the performance appraisal system can have a profound impact on the ability to achieve the vision. Initially, professional development will be most likely delivered by an external consultant. But this, in the long term, is not financially sustainable and a team of 'internal consultants' will eventually be skilled enough to manage the programme for the most part. Details of the kinds of skills needed across the restorative continuum are detailed in Appendix 5.

- Where particular staff members are resisting the changes, despite plenty of effective support and opportunities for skill development, then they must be held accountable (in a restorative way of course) for their behaviour – what's good for holding students accountable must hold for staff as well. It may well be the case that ongoing resistance to the new vision may mean that performance management processes have eventually to be triggered. However, as Heath and Heath (2010) warn us, it may be that what looks like resistance is actually caused by a lack of clarity about expectations and direction, so careful reflection on how the change process is proceeding might be needed.

- Staff might have to be let go, if a restructuring is to occur. Sometimes staff will voluntarily resign or request a transfer if they are at such odds with the new way of doing business. Fierce, honest, restorative conversations with staff who are disengaged or refusing to buy in to the vision will become necessary, and these require skill and courage from those in leadership positions. It will also pay, if resistance is widespread, to take some time to review the transformation by checking through the steps so far to determine if a step or two has been rushed or not completed properly. Since successful completion of each step is the basis for the next, it holds that there might be pieces missing. It will be worth going back.

- Where recruitment of leadership and middle management is occurring, selection needs to include a clear charter about delivering the changes that the vision demands. It will be important that, as far as is possible, new staff members' values are aligned with the school's values. How relational are they in their attitudes, particularly to disciplinary matters? How well will they fit into the new vision?

- Do current job descriptions and role statements match the vision? Do these need some work to align them with the vision? Does the job of middle manager change from someone who doles out punishments on behalf of classroom teachers, or does the role now mean facilitation of problem-solving and healing of relationships? These changes need to be clearly communicated to everyone and backed up by senior management.

- It will be very important to recognise the efforts of the implementation team, and the staff who are making the changes that are making a difference. Both private and public recognition go a long way to maintaining motivation when school life is already so very busy. Recognition may sometimes involve granting permission to visit other schools, or attending regional, national or international conferences. In our experience, though, a simple word of thanks or encouragement – verbal or written – counts a great deal.

Step 6 Generating Short-term Wins

Without some early successes, motivation can fail and cynics' 'I told you this wouldn't work' will ring from the rafters. This can be profoundly discouraging, so planning for early wins is vital. Creating short-term targets is an important first step. The implementation team needs to choose something that is highly visible, unambiguous, likely to succeed, and urgent if possible. Kotter and Cohen (2002; as cited in Heath and Heath 2010) have observed that in most successful change, the change process in individuals is a sequence of 'see–feel–change' (p.106). The message here is that wins are not random events. Short-term wins that are publicly acknowledged and celebrated give practitioners hope, maintain motivation and influence critics and cynics in positive ways. Some examples of short-term wins might include changes in:

- suspensions/fixed-term exclusions/stand-downs
- referrals to middle managers
- playground incidents
- detentions
- bullying incidents
- wellbeing surveys.

Opportunities for staff to share stories in staff and faculty meetings allow good news stories to infect both converts and cynics. Understanding what it is that is producing the positive changes is also important, so all staff can make the links.

Chapter 12

Implementing and Embedding Change

The key steps covered in this chapter are:

1. Step 7 Keeping the pressure on

2. Step 8 Maintaining the gains

We reminded readers at the beginning of this section of the book that sustained change takes years, not months, that we have to be in it for the long haul. In thinking about declaring victory too soon, we are reminded of George W. Bush's famous remarks[1] about the end of major combat operations in the second Iraq war in May 2003, creating an illusion that the greater part of the job had been done. How wrong he and his administration were. Please don't think that culture change is about winning a war, but we wanted to paint a vivid picture about premature declarations!

So many schools we visit think they have done the job of achieving culture change when in fact they have been tinkering around the edges with first order changes (see Section 2) or have taken their foot off the pedal or have dropped the handles of the wheelbarrow. In these final stages, like the last stages of a marathon, we need to stay motivated and focused. But marathons finish. Culture change actually doesn't. There is no end to the journey. If you want to create a new habit of mind, of behaviour, it requires focus and repetition. Without both, things will go back to the way they were. To help with that, we have two last steps, Keeping the Pressure On and Maintaining the Gains.

---

1   The whole difficult issue that occurred as a result of this speech on board an aircraft carrier and a banner stating 'Mission Accomplished' in the background of the official photos on the day of the declaration of victory can be found at http://en.wikipedia.org/wiki/2003_Mission_Accomplished_speech.

Step 7 Keeping the Pressure On

Letting go of the wheelbarrow at this stage is *extremely dangerous*. Kotter (2007, p.8) reminds us of the dangers of declaring victory too soon:

> But it is the premature victory celebration that kills momentum. And then the powerful forces associated with tradition take over... Instead of declaring victory, leaders of successful efforts use the credibility afforded by short-term wins to tackle even bigger problems. They go after systems and structures that are not consistent with the transformation vision and have not been confronted before. They pay great attention to who is promoted, who is hired, and how people are developed. They include new reengineering projects that are even bigger in scope than the initial ones. They understand that renewal efforts take not months but years.

Change needs to be driven deeply into the fabric of the school culture so that it becomes part of the school's DNA. By the very hierarchical nature of a school, it can be very resilient (Lee 2004), and it will very quickly slip back into old ways of doing business – within the space of a year or two, unless concrete steps are taken to maximise and leverage the reforms. We have seen this time and time again when key people who have had responsibility for the implementation of RP leave a school, only to see an almost immediate revert to type in behaviour. We also have seen the heartbreak that occurs when a new principal/head teacher is appointed to a school who has no real understanding of the work that has been done to achieve the current restorative culture, nor have they any real deep relationship knowledge and skill. This can undo a restorative culture in the space of a year or two. Change is constant and so is the need to sustain and plan for departures in key personnel and the appointments of new ones.

Here are some suggestions:

- Broaden the scope of the projects: involve more year levels; offer workshops for parents; train teams of student/pupil facilitators; turn attention to using RP for staff conflict resolution and performance management; experiment with restorative processes for absentee/attendance issues; provide ongoing high quality skill development – not once, but twice, three times and more; broaden the use of RP for all sorts of issues, limited only by the imagination (including restorative farewells to expelled students/pupils).

- Turn attention to *developmental* projects such as the use of circles in classrooms to build social and emotional competence in learners if this is not already happening. This will act in a preventative way to build capacity amongst students and teachers to problem-solve together. This becomes the fence at the top of the cliff to prevent students from falling over.

- Keep up the acknowledgements and announcements around improvements that are becoming evident – consistent proof that new ways of 'doing' are working.

- After each success/win, analyse what worked and what didn't, and how the situation could be improved, involving key stakeholders (leadership, staff, students, parents).

- Take great care with the recruitment of new staff, especially senior and middle managers. We have both witnessed the decay of a deeply positive restorative/relational culture by the selection of entirely the wrong person in a key leadership position, and it is heartbreaking for the implementation team and the wider school community. The school's governing body needs to ensure that these decisions are made with culture change momentum in mind.

- Give a range of staff from across the school community responsibilities for new projects. This develops leadership and increases the likelihood of ongoing buy-in.

- Bring in new blood to the implementation team with their fresh ideas and opportunities to develop leadership.

- Engage with the agencies and organisations that are also involved with families and children (police, children and young people services, family services, housing, local county, councils, authorities, health) so that a whole community approach to problem-solving might be explored.

It is in this dangerous stage of implementation that the role of leadership again becomes critical – leading for *long-term* change, rather than leading the school out of a crisis or urgency around the need for change. We think this is the least 'sexy' part of the change process and interest and excitement must be kept high in deliberate ways with new projects and inspirational visionary leadership.

Another important element that we see missing sadly in many schools is the capacity of the leadership team to develop leadership in *others*, and then for staff to influence each other. It is how the big 'L' leaders in the school encourage, nurture and support small 'l' leadership throughout the school (Kotter 2012a). Schools that have been successful in sustaining practice have created leadership throughout their school, with young and inspiring teachers taking the lead on implementation and sharing practice. They have a strong voice in what happens and in turn are far more accountable for what happens in their school.

Step 8 Maintaining the Gains

It seems counter-intuitive that culture change occurs at Step 8 of the change process, but there are no guarantees of this unless the changes are firmly embedded as 'the way things are done around here'. This does not happen by chance or good luck, and it is vital that a strategic approach remains in place. We firmly believe that there is no final destination that is reached where we can gasp, 'Job done. Time to put our feet up.' The pressure to maintain the changes (like eating sensibly and staying fit) must be kept up, and in some ways it's the ongoing journey towards the vision that counts, especially as school communities and societies are constantly evolving.

Some ideas for maintaining progress look very like Step 7, but have to be relentless to be effective:

- Talk up the gains that have been made at every opportunity and join the dots between these successes and the use of restorative approaches. Talk about why performance is improving. Do not assume that staff, parents and pupils can make those links for themselves.

- Continue with a robust programme of learning and growth and make no assumptions that everyone is now unconsciously competent. Remember that it takes focus and practice to create new habits.

- Continue to recruit and promote the next generation of people who are committed to the values and vision of the school and the culture change process.

- Continue to hold those who are not stepping up to the mark accountable for their behaviours (again, in a restorative way).

- Be aware that every year there is a new group of staff, students and parents who will need careful induction into the school culture.

- Showcase your gains to other schools and stay abreast of what is happening nationally and internationally. Each time we go to a conference with RP as a focus we both come back inspired with the gains that others have made and learn from their experiences. This will keep the implementation team motivated to continue.

- Continue to build awareness and collaboration in and with the wider community.

In some ways, it's almost like beginning the culture change process all over again.

We have offered in these eight steps the best advice we can find from change experts, and where possible we have adapted these into some concrete strategies that will be useful for your implementation team. It will take your focus, determination, vision, leadership, honesty and courage to see the changes through. At times you will feel utterly exhausted, frustrated and discouraged; the odds will seem insurmountable; your team might fall out with each other; you might get a new boss who doesn't remotely understand RP. Sounds scary? It can be. It can also be exhilarating and deeply satisfying to see young people respond positively and staff change their behaviour, and parents grateful that you have taken the time with their family. It can make you proud to be part of a school community that is identified as caring yet strong with high standards of academic achievement *and* staff and student welfare.

If one of the values that drive the work you do is to make a difference, then being part of the implementation team bent on serious culture change can become your vehicle. But the road ahead needs a map, and the eight steps are just that.

Conclusion

If you have come this far in reading the book, our hats are off to you for your sheer persistence and we hope it pays off for you! It has taken both of us many years to appreciate the difference between hearing about a great idea, using it and seeing it work and training others, through to helping and witnessing the capacity for that idea to transform the culture of an organisation like a school. It's an idea, this one called Restorative Practice, whose time has come. We need to understand how to harness this idea, to become skilled at it, to embed this idea into the heads and hearts of others, so it doesn't disappear once we move on. Far from being merely a tool to help schools manage behaviour and for students to resolve conflict, this is a skill for life and a way of thinking about our relationships with others if we are to be effective friends, neighbours, partners, workers, leaders, managers, team mates and parents.

We've covered some major territory, and like other authors before us, we worry about what we've left out, what we've left in, what will have changed by the time you are reading this. We've explored very briefly what the practice of restorative justice looks like in a school community. We've looked at the complex world of organisational and culture change – how it affects all of us: what will work, and what won't. And lastly, we've broken down the organisational change process into manageable bites that we hope can keep you organised and hopeful and optimistic that your efforts will not be wasted.

And why should we bother? Because the school is above all the one place in a community where pretty much everyone goes. It is also the place where we both believe educators can achieve much more than just a decent education for our young people. Schools can, with inspirational leadership and the right philosophical approach, be the centre of peace-building for our families and the wider community – perhaps, if we are all committed (and why not), world peace!

We hope that this book will inspire educators, school leaders and school communities to pave the way for a brighter future for our young people, and, ultimately, everyone.

Appendix 1
Eight Step Planning Grid
Getting Ready for Change[1]

The following planning grid has been designed to help you and your implementation team plan for successful implementation and to review when progress has stalled.

The planning grid consists of three stages, each containing a number of steps, described in detail in Section 3 of this book.

Stage	Steps
Stage 1: Getting ready for change	1. Making a case for change
	2. Putting an implementation team together
	3. Creating a vision for the future
Stage 2: Overcoming inertia and getting the ball rolling	4. Communicating the vision to capture hearts and minds
	5. Overcoming obstacles and getting the ball rolling
	6. Generating short term wins
Stage 3: Implementing and embedding change	7. Keeping the pressure on
	8. Maintaining the gains

The grid consists of six columns from left to right within the three areas of the change process outlining the:

- Step

- Area for planning

1   Adapted from www.kotterinternational.com.

- Possible tasks

- Breakdown of tasks

- Team led by

- By when (and measurement).

Possible tasks have been provided to assist with planning. You might add to these or develop your own. You then want to consider who will lead the task and timelines. You might also consider how this can be measured, that is, what will have happened to show the task has been completed.

You might start at the beginning of the grid or where you think your school is in the change process. Either way, we recommend that you review all areas to ensure that you have not missed a critical area.

Stage 1: Getting Ready for Change

Step	Area	Possible tasks	Breakdown of tasks	Team led by	By when and how to measure
1. Making a case for change	Identify key people to do some ground work

Identify potential threats

Identify opportunities

Begin to engage with stakeholders (staff, students, parents, governing bodies) | Select a small group to do start up work

Use and interrogate data

Identify imperatives

Do a SWOT/SOAR/FFA audit

Feed data back to stakeholders and engage in robust dialogue around issues | | | |

| 2. Putting an implementation team together | Putting a team together | Call for expressions of interest (be selective)

Shoulder tap where necessary

Check for spread of skills, weaknesses | | | |
| | Team building | Do some serious team building to get team to commit at an emotional level | | | |

cont.

Stage 1: Getting Ready for Change

Step	Area	Possible tasks	Breakdown of tasks	Team led by	By when and how to measure
3. Creating a vision for the future	Develop a short summary that captures the future	Team to work on this			
	Determine the values that are central to the change	Explore and adapt current values statements (define values as behaviours)			
	Create a strategy to launch and execute the vision	Create or realign the current school strategy to fit the 'new' vision			
		Launch the vision			
	Guiding coalition becomes fluent with the vision	Practice to become fluent			

4. Communicating the vision to capture hearts and minds	Talk often about the change vision	Use every opportunity/setting to speak about the changes			
	Address concerns and anxieties	Structure regular exercises to raise issues			
		Listen carefully. Get back to staff with suggestions			
	Tie everything back to the vision	All decisions and activities are tied to the vision			
	Lead by example – communicate by words and deeds	Talk the talk and walk the talk			

cont.

Stage 2: Overcoming Inertia and Getting the Ball Rolling

Step	Area	Possible tasks	Breakdown of tasks	Team led by	By when and how to measure
5. Removing obstacles and empowering action	Get rid of obstacles that impede the vision	Identify people within the organisation and/or recruit people whose job it is to deliver the changes			
	Encourage risk taking, non-traditional ideas, activities and actions				
	Develop Skills	Develop a programme of professional development			
	Choose the vision over self-interest	Recognise and reward those making the changes			
	Changes structures and systems that undermine the vision	Check structures, operations, role descriptions performance to make sure they fit with the vision			

	Remove barriers – process to be consistent with the vision/values, behaviours and accountabilities		
6. Generating short-term wins	Look for sure fire projects that don't require support of critics	Choose project that is urgent, has wide support and is likely to succeed	
	Choose early targets that will deliver (pros and cons); not too "expensive" and can't fail		
	Acknowledge and reward staff who have helped meet targets	Constant reassurance/nurturing, celebrating the wins, keeping everyone in the loop about what is working	

cont.

Stage 3: Implementing and Embedding Change

Step	Area	Possible tasks	Breakdown of tasks	Team led by	By when and how to measure
7. Keeping the pressure on	Using increased credibility to make further changes for everything that doesn't fit the vision	After every win, analyse what went right and what needs improving Set new goals			
	Hiring, promoting and developing people who can implement the change vision	Continuous improvement			
	Reinvigorate with new changes	Add new blood to change team			

8. Maintaining Gains	Using stakeholder feedback and achievement data to change behaviour	Talk about progress at every chance and acknowledge specific behaviours which have created more effective performance
	Improve and widen leadership	Encouraging leadership throughout the ranks
	Maintain the pressure on values and behaviours	Include change ideals and values when hiring and training new staff
		Public recognition of key members of original team
		Create succession plans for key leaders moving on

Appendix 2
Readiness for Change Checklist

The following checklist is designed to assist the leadership and implementation team to determine school readiness for the implementation of restorative practices. We look first at broader environmental factors to determine the issue of readiness and then whether you need to be embarking on first or second order change.

What is it That You Want to Achieve?

The first step is to be clear about what it is that you are embarking on. Does the school already have a relational culture, where the restorative philosophy would be a good fit and will meet with little resistance? In order for you to make this assessment, we offer a comprehensive checklist developed from Section 1 of this book. If your answers indicate there are minimal gaps, then first order change might be all that is needed to begin the process of RP implementation. If the gaps are sizeable, then second order change may be necessary and there are some serious questions that must be answered in order for you to be clear about what's ahead.

Please work through the following list with a colleague or group of interested others. There are some further questions for you at the completion of the checklist.

Values, Attitudes and Climate	Notes
☐ The attitude to learning and behaviour from both teachers and learners is unfailingly positive. ☐ Difficult moments are regarded as educational opportunities, indeed, as teachable moments. ☐ The school values are clearly defined for adults, students and parents in terms of expected behaviours and these behaviours are explicit, taught, known and modelled by all adults.	

☐ Offending behaviour is viewed as a breach of relationships, against school community values.

☐ There is an inclusive approach to teaching and behaviour with the system aiming to keep students at school. There is an attitude of persistence among staff, parents and students that means that the school is unwilling to give up on difficult students or to want to get rid of them at the earliest opportunity.

☐ Young people are not demonised. The school sees its role as a partner in child rearing with families – not always an equal partnership, but the school is prepared to step up nevertheless.

☐ The school is the hub of its local community both physically and metaphorically. Strong, positive, collaborative relationships are evident between the school, local police, local authorities/councils, local agencies, local businesses and community groups.

☐ There is a whole of community approach to tackling the issues for young people and their families. This is seen as a shared responsibility and a challenge that the school embraces, rather than shies away from.

☐ There is a recognition that, and commitment to, the notion that positive, robust relationships lie at the heart of learning and pedagogical practice, of wellbeing and a sense of belonging and connectedness; and all decisions, structures, policies and procedures reflect this understanding.

☐ There is an understanding of the need to restore relationships in the aftermath of conflict and wrongdoing or major incidents within the school. This is reflected in practice with the focus of problem-solving around the damage that needs to be fixed rather the rule breach that needs to be punished and is solution-focused.

☐ There is a comfortable marriage between the values of the school and the values of a restorative approach to problem-solving. Leadership is values-based and transformational, and leaders walk the talk, and model the required change.

cont.

Values, Attitudes and Climate	Notes
☐ The school regards itself as a learning organisation, committed to continual improvement. Data is used effectively to inform discussion, debate and problem-solving. Data is used to address gaps and reality is regularly interrogated. ☐ Visitors to the school are treated with respect, approached with a friendly greeting from students and adults, and are made to feel welcome. There is a high level of trust evident across and between members of the school and wider community. ☐ The school *feels* friendly, peaceful and polite. The school has a reputation for a focus on the positives, for its use of fair process, for academic excellence, for making a difference in the community. Enrolments might be increasing, rather than diminishing, and car park and supermarket conversations amongst parents about the school are positive. ☐ Everyone understands that the school community is never static, that the school membership is constantly altering and that what has worked for one cohort of students may not work for the next. The school is proactive, future-focused, and welcomes change. ☐ There is clear and effective dialogue from the top down, bottom up and between staff, students, parents and anyone engaged with the school community.	
Links with Curriculum and Teaching and Learning	**Notes**
☐ Clear linkages between key initiatives, system imperatives, pedagogy and key competencies can be made with RP so it will not seen as an add-on or stand-alone initiative. The approach is viewed as a possible enhancement of the core business of teaching and learning within the school community – a framework for best practice.	

☐ As part of relationship skill development, teachers are skilled in basic effective, innovative classroom management and pedagogy.

☐ Attention is paid to the quality of the relationships between learners as well as between teacher and learner, in recognition of the need for an optimal environment for learning – a sense of safety and belonging.

☐ The school has a stimulating emotional environment where interest and enjoyment are maximised for learners and teachers alike. Impediments to this are appropriately addressed.

☐ The behaviour of learners is not seen as a separate issue to be managed outside the curriculum. Regular class meetings are held to develop social and emotional competencies, self-regulation and whole-of-class responsibility for the climate in the classroom.

☐ There is effective communication and collaboration between pastoral care and curriculum roles (e.g. classroom teachers, deans, heads of house, syndicate leaders and heads of faculty/department) when behaviour issues arise in classrooms.

☐ Induction for new staff and learners is taken seriously and adequately resourced. There is a prominent focus on a positive blame-free approach to problem-solving.

☐ Transitions for learners are well managed; between schools, within school from one year level to the next or between sub-schools, and subject changes so that a strong sense of connectedness and/or closure is an outcome.

☐ A case management approach is taken to address issues around particular learners, with preparedness to work on underlying issues as well as the symptomatic behaviours. The school is well connected to providers that can assist with student and family issues.

☐ Relational competence is built into the school's appraisal, selection and recruitment processes.

cont.

Restorative/Relational Practice	Notes

☐ There will be some practice that already exists that can be regarded as 'restorative' – practice that has a strong relational focus.
 ☐ There is a well-developed continuum of 'disciplinary' practice, understood by all members of the school community, that can be adapted readily to situations from serious to minor.
 ☐ There is a whole school approach to a relational philosophy and a consistency of practice across the whole school (teachers, support staff and school administration) so that everyone trusts the systems in place.
 ☐ Practice addresses the harm from inappropriate behaviour and incidents in a way that:
    ☐ deals with conflict and disruption in a timely manner
    ☐ repairs harm in the aftermath of wrongdoing
    ☐ addresses issues with all involved
    ☐ works with those involved to find the best solution for what has happened
    ☐ embraces a diversity of solutions by understanding there may be many ways to solve a problem
    ☐ focuses on what needs to happen to repair harm.
    ☐ looks at what needs to happen to prevent further harm.
 ☐ The overall focus is on developing positive relationships between students, teachers, parents and the wider community.
 ☐ Energy is spent on developing social and emotional competence and positive behaviours so that young people have the capacity to engage effectively in problem-solving.
 ☐ Both practice and practitioners are reflective and the school is intent on developing best practice. With a combination of positive pressure and support, the adults are held accountable for their practice as professionals.	

□ Leaders and middle managers lead by example with this approach.

□ Learners are taught about the approaches to problem-solving so that they can actively and effectively participate; eventually there is evidence that they are using this approach to solve their own problems at school and at home; parents are comfortable to approach the school when there is a problem.

□ Practice is adapted for particular settings within the school community (early years, primary, middle years, secondary and beyond, special needs, alternate settings).

□ Staff conflict is acknowledged and acted on with a restorative approach, with all adults having a clear understanding of the need to model what we want from young people. We must be prepared to use the same approach for the issues that arise for us. If the school does not have enough skill to manage such issues, then it must be prepared to access external help.

□ There is an alignment of philosophy, policy and practice. Any behaviour management policy is framed in more positive terms such as 'Relationship' policy, 'Care and Responsibility' policy or 'Respect' policy.

□ Dialogue about learners, their families or staff issues shifts from blame to flexible problem-solving evidenced in practice, language and actions. Problems are seen as opportunities to refine existing practice.

□ *Everyone's* voice is important, not just the voice of adults within the school community. There is more *listening* and less *telling*.

□ The school is very clear about what *is* negotiable and what *isn't* in terms of rules, limits and boundaries in classrooms and playgrounds – the learner experiences the school and the adults as firm, fair and flexible and the rules make sense to children and adults alike. Boundaries are generated and abandoned as needed.

cont.

Restorative/Relational Practice	Notes
☐ Roles have been re-negotiated around *who is responsible* for managing behaviour and learning issues to increase the involvement and responsibility of classroom teachers. The person who owns the relationship with the troublesome student is central to the problem-solving and healing the relationship is a strong focus. Middle managers are expected to take a relational approach to problem-solving and this is built into their role statements.	
☐ The issue of zero tolerance is viewed as: 'we don't accept that behaviour in our school', rather than one of excluding students based on their behaviour as the default response. An incident signals deeper issues and the school is prepared to work with those involved to resolve these issues where possible.	
☐ Professional development for adults takes a high priority and is resourced to reflect this; not only around responding to new curriculum and system imperatives, but keeping 'relationships' front and centre, and there is balance between these two often-competing pressures.	
☐ Collegial, professional relationships among staff have been developed and the dialogue reflects 'the problem is the problem' rather than regarding difficult behaviours with deficit thinking and pathologising of young people and their families. Language used is solution-focused and avoids blame.	
☐ Older students are skilled up to help sort lower-level/minor issues with younger students, supported by the adults in the school ready to step in if a matter requires their attention. Students do not do the work of the adults.	
☐ Attention is paid to follow-up, data collection and analysis. There is a data driven approach to problem-solving that is aimed at school improvement and addressing gaps in learning, behaviour and practice.	

☐ In the case of performance issues, a relational approach is the first option, before more serious sanctions become necessary. Problems are not left to fester and/or escalate.	

It is our view that *first order change* around the implementation of restorative practice is only successful in building sustainable practice when the environment is conducive to change. This requires a strong relational focus that is values driven and the implementation of restorative practices is aligned with a school vision that is relational in nature.

If your answers to the checklist indicated large gaps, then *second order change*, which involves a rather more complex change management effort, might be a better option. The school actually has to do something significantly or fundamentally different from what is currently happening. The process is deemed irreversible, as once begun it is difficult to return to the way things were.

Considerations in embarking on second order change include:

- Is there agreement that change is necessary?

- Is there a mandate for change (within school, board, Department/Ministry, etc.)?

- How urgent is the identified need?

- Have you conducted an audit of what is currently happening in the school?

- Is the school emotionally healthy, or is it an emotionally expensive environment with high staff turnover, or falling enrolments due to school culture?

- Do you have the financial and people resources to make change happen?

- Do you have at least 75 per cent of the senior leadership prepared to support a change process?

- Are decision-makers knowledgeable about research on teaching, learning, and student development?

- Are decision-makers committed to supporting both formal and informal leadership and to the critical role each plays in effecting change?

- Is there an implementation team, or at least the beginnings of one?

- To what extent are the school values known and practised? Do they align with relational practice?

- What is your relationship like with other schools in your cluster? Is there a relationship?

- What do you see as the impediments or barriers to change?

At this point, you should be clearer about whether or not your efforts will be focused on trialling restorative practice on a small scale to build support for larger-scale change, or boots-and-all second order change. Whatever your assessment, Section 3 of this book should help guide you through careful steps for managing the change process effectively.

Other considerations might include:

- Do you have enough staff that will pick up on new practice quickly (Early Adopters)?

- Are staff used to sharing practice?

- To what extent is there a culture of student and family blaming?

- To what extent are the staff up to date on the research into brain development and function?

- Do staff believe in the capacity of a child to change their behaviour?

- What are the social/emotional competencies of management and staff? How relational are they?

- Are there any pockets of conflict within the staff that haven't been resolved?

- To what extent is there effective family involvement/ engagement? How willing are parents to come to the school?

- Is there an understanding of what long-term poverty does to people and their values (if your school draws attention from a low socio-economic area).

Appendix 3
Audit Tools[1]

SWOT Analysis

The SWOT Analysis, similar to the Force Field Analysis, is a tool that is a part of the strategic planning process and is a method used to evaluate the *Strengths, Weaknesses, Opportunities* and *Threats* involved in achieving your statement of purpose. It allows a process that starts with a brainstorming process to develop understanding and discussion, that leads to decision-making and alignment around a 3–5 year approach.

It was originally developed because much business planning back in the 1960s and 1970s failed. Through research developed from the Stanford Research Institute, it was agreed that the reason that this happened was that *it was difficult for a team of people to agree on, manage and commit to a comprehensive set of actions over a long period.* Think of your own situations – when you are busy and in the middle of term thinking about what else needs to be accomplished, your focus isn't exactly strongly attached to 'What is this school going to look like and feel like in three years?' Long-term planning requires a complete mindset change and a commitment to that change.

So the SWOT Analysis (through a brainstorming process) enables proactive thinking and is usually set out in a four-box diagram, as outlined below and generally answers the questions in each of the four areas in the template. Also refer to the worksheet on Mind Tools, www.mindtools.com/pages/article/worksheets/SWOT Analysis Worksheet.pdf.

You will also find generally that the strengths and weakness will be far greater than opportunities and threats, but it is still important

---

1   The FFA process on p.201 was adapted from Richmond (2009).

to consider them when you are planning towards the achievement of long-term outcomes.

STRENGTHS	WEAKNESSES
Attributes we have in achieving our statement of purpose	*Attributes we have that are harmful in achieving our purpose*
What do you do well?	What could you improve?
What unique resources can you draw on?	Where do you have fewer resources than others?
What do others see as your strengths?	What are others likely to see as weaknesses?
Example:	Example:
• Advantages of the RP approach • Capabilities to achieve this • The appeal to parents, students and staff in this approach • Strong resources and people • Experience, knowledge and data that support this • Financial reserves – likely returns • Innovative aspects • School quality/culture • Processes and systems that support this • Attitudinal and behavioural strengths • Management support	• Disadvantages of the approach • Gaps in capabilities • What won't appeal to parents, students and staff? • Weak resources and people • Experience or knowledge that does not support this • Lack of financial viability to support the change • Effects or distractions on core educational pursuits • Processes and systems that will need to change • Lack of commitment • Lack of leadership from the SLT and/or HODs

OPPORTUNITIES	THREATS
External conditions that are helpful in achieving our purpose	*External conditions that could damage the achievement of our statement of purpose*
What opportunities are open to you?	What trends could do you harm?
What trends could you take advantage of?	What are other schools doing (competition)?
How can you turn your strengths into opportunities?	What threats do your weaknesses expose you to?
For example:	For example:
• Global research on RP outcomes	• Legislative impacts
• Information and research	• Distraction from core activities
• Partnerships with other RP schools	• New contradictive ideas
• Student and parent responses to the new approach	• Obstacles faced
• Current trends to schooling approaches	• Insurmountable weaknesses
	• Attacks from 'powers above' or other schools

Other resources are available on the internet – see, for example, SWOT Analysis (Wikipedia) and businessballs.com.

SOAR Analysis

This process is similar to the SWOT analysis (a four-quadrant set of questions, adapted from Stavros and Hinrichs 2009 – see Further Reading) having a more positive appreciative enquiry focus with questions about aspirations and results, rather than weaknesses and threats – a more strengths-based strategy. A broad base of stakeholders (beyond the senior leadership team) is engaged to discover the school's strengths and opportunities in order to create shared aspirations, goals, strategies and a commitment to achieving results. This group is broader than students, parents, staff and the governing body and will include the wider community such as other schools, providers of services to the school and local businesses.

'The conversations focus on what an organisation is doing right, what skills could be enhanced, and what is compelling to those who have a 'stake' in the organisation's success' (Stavros and Hinrichs 2009, p.9). While the focus is positive, weaknesses and threats are not ignored, and are addressed in the opportunities and results conversations. It will be important to identify all the stakeholders who will be impacted on by the success of the school and include them (or at least their representatives) in the brainstorming process.

The SOAR process is intended initially for small groups to promote engagement and safe expression of ideas for participants. The results of these conversations are fed back to a larger group to build a shared understanding and can be done at any level in the school, and involve any number of participants, including those via virtual connection.

STRENGTHS	OPPORTUNITIES
What can we build on?	*What are our stakeholders asking for?*
• What are we most proud of? How does this reflect our greatest strength? • What makes us unique? What can we be the best at? Is there anything we already do that is world class? • What is our proudest achievement in the last year or two? • How do we use our strengths to get results? • How do our strengths fit with the current realities and demands of the system, and our competition (other schools)?	• What opportunities exist that are provided by external forces and trends? • What are our top three opportunities on which to focus our efforts? • How can we best meet the needs of our stakeholders? • Who are our possible new students, parents, staff? • How can we be distinctively different from our competitors? Who are our new markets and what can we offer them? • How can we reframe challenges as opportunities? What are the challenges? • What new skills to we need to move forward?

ASPIRATIONS	RESULTS
What do we care deeply about?	*How do we know we are succeeding?*
• When we explore our values, what are we passionate about? • Reflecting on our strengths and opportunities, who are we? Who should we become? Where should we be going? • What is our most compelling aspiration? • What strategic initiatives/ projects would support our aspirations?	• Considering all our SOAs, what measures would be meaningful to know we are on track with our goals? • What would be 3–5 indicators that we are on track (data; staff, student, parent satisfaction)? • What resources are needed to implement our most vital projects? • What are the best rewards to support those who achieve our goals?

For more detailed understanding of and instruction on this process we recommend www.soar-strategy.com.

Force Field Analysis (FFA)

The Force Field Analysis, originally developed in 1943 by Kurt Lewin, is used as a process to facilitate problem-solving when working with a group of people who want to achieve a particular outcome such as the implementing a particular restorative practice (RP) process, e.g. referral to withdrawal or Time-Out room. The three components in the model are the:

1. goal

2. facilitating forces, and

3. blocking forces.

These are two parts to this process: Part A, involving the identification of the goals; and Part B, concerned with the facilitating and blocking forces.

Part A: Identifying what you are addressing and what you want to achieve

The goal/goals

In terms of RP, the goal can be short, medium or long-term, related to embedding the RP philosophy, and is best developed using available data that can be used to help shape and measure realistic outcomes. Whatever the outcome, *it needs to be clearly defined.* For example:

- reducing the current levels of referral to the withdrawal room by half – rather than seeking to eliminate them altogether in a short period of time, or

- use of Circle Time by *all* teachers might become 75 per cent of all Year 9 teachers using circles by the end of the second term. Reaching consensus around goals will be an important first step in the FFA process.

Part B. Identifying the facilitating and blocking forces

The process of identifying facilitating and blocking forces is part of an audit process. This will validate what is being done well, and also the untapped potential that can be harnessed. It is also vital to identify the blocking forces, so that there can be some problem-solving to reduce and/or eliminate those forces that reduce the likelihood of the goal being achieved.

FACILITATING FORCES   BLOCKING FORCES   GOAL

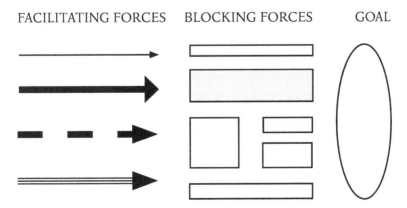

FACILITATING FORCES

In the diagram, the facilitating forces (or existing strengths) are represented by a range of arrows of differing widths. The differences in width represent the relative strengths of each force, where some will have a greater capacity to influence the achievement of the goals than others. This will help planners think through what needs to be strengthened, and can be used to consult with stakeholders to harvest their ideas about 'how to' to build on what already exists in a way that leverages off what is already working. For example:

- there may be a strong 'relational' approach already in the school, and strong values around community and respect, so that doing RP will not be a big stretch, or

- the senior leadership team is already on board and happy to listen to suggestions about resourcing.

BLOCKING FORCES

The FFA process has identified three types of blocking forces: *givens, reducibles* and *removables*.

1. *Givens* are those things that cannot be changed such as the socio-economic status because of the school's geographic location.

2. *Reducibles* are the blockers that can, with some careful and imaginative planning, be reduced. For example, a pattern of increased disruption in the lunch hour might be improved if it is realised that students with too much time on their hands 'get up to no good'. If the morning break is extended and the lunch break shortened, and interesting activities devised to engage students are introduced, some of the issues can be 'structured out'. Exposing staff to the data and the problems means their help can be enlisted to come up with creative solutions.

3. *Removables* are the blockers that can be eliminated entirely, as the following examples suggest:

- If the overuse of deans/year level co-ordinators to supervise detentions for teaching staff is an issue and identified as a blocker, then a change in policy may pull the practice up short. If teaching staff wish to use detentions, they may do so, but have to supervise them themselves. They are no longer permitted to ask others to do that for them. This will relieve the deans of the burden and allow them to focus on more serious welfare issues.

- Another example might be that parents are reluctant to engage in school activities such as teacher interviews held in the evenings. With some creativity (thinking outside the square) by teachers and students together, these events can become overwhelmingly productive and vastly improve engagement between parents and the school community.

The efforts of the planning/implementation team are to work on weakening the wall of blockers and increase the positive facilitating forces.

Further reading

There are other versions of the FFA process available on the web. A Google search reveals quite a few. You might like to check out www.mindtools.com/pages/article/newTED_06.htm.

Appendix 4
Sample Detention Survey

Adapted from Corrigan (2009).

This is a sample of a simple review instrument developed to establish whether or not a particular protocol (detention) is delivering the outcomes a school staff might believe it does. Other protocol reviews can be developed along similar lines and we suggest simple online surveys (e.g. Survey Monkey) are used so that collating responses is very simple. You might think it useful to survey parents of those students who turn up in detentions as well.

Administering the Survey to Students

Use this survey with students who have had more than one detention in the last year. The school is interested in how well detentions work – for the school and for students. We're interested in what students think.

Some students will need help reading or understanding the language. Please offer help, via a senior student or adult, but don't lead them to any particular answers. The results from a cohort of 'detention' students will need to be collated. Say to the student (s):

> There are no right or wrong answers, and you won't get in trouble for honest answers. Just read the question, think, and give us an honest answer. Please don't put your name on the form. We are interested to know what you really think about the detention system and will give you some feedback once we have collated the results.

Administering the Survey to Staff

Use this survey to establish staff views about whether or not they believe the detention system is delivering hoped-for outcomes.

This survey can be completed at a staff meeting or set up to be done online as suggested above. Explain that the student voice is being gathered as well, and that results of both surveys will be fed back at the next possible opportunity. No names required.

Feedback to Stakeholders

Comparisons can be made with both sets of results to see whether or not adults and young people share the same views about the purpose and outcomes of the detention protocol. When both sets of results are fed back to staff (and students), allow plenty of time for discussion about the meaning and implications of these results. It will help an analysis of what's working and what isn't. Why not try this in small groups of staff seated in circles, so everyone has a voice. One might finish such an exercise with a question: Does detention have a place in our school, and if it does, how might we improve it in line with our restorative philosophy?

Teacher Voice: Detention Survey

Tick a box	Strongly Agree	Agree	Disagree	Strongly Disagree
1. Giving a detention tells students that I take bad behaviour seriously.				
2. Doing a detention helps students think about the things they did wrong.				
3. Detentions are good for helping students improve their behaviour.				
4. Kids deserve every detention I give.				

cont.

Tick a box	Strongly Agree	Agree	Disagree	Strongly Disagree
5. They don't mind doing a detention if they deserve it.				
6. They skip detentions where they can.				
7. Detentions remind students that the adults at school are in charge.				
8. Some teachers give lots of detentions and others give out very few.				
9. When students have done the detention, it removes any bad feelings between me and the student.				
10. Students are better behaved for teachers that give out lots of detentions.				
11. Detentions are a good way to make sure our school is a safe school.				
12. What suggestions do you have that might improve the effectiveness of the detention as an intervention to develop better behaviours for learning?				

Student Voice: Detention Survey

Tick a box	Strongly Agree	Agree	Disagree	Strongly Disagree
1. Doing a detention tells me that the school takes bad behaviour seriously.				
2. Doing a detention helps me think about the things I did wrong.				
3. Detentions are good for helping me improve my behaviour.				
4. I don't deserve most of the detentions I get.				
5. I don't mind doing a detention if I deserve it.				
6. I skip detentions where I can.				
7. Detentions make me think that the adults at school are in charge.				
8. Some teachers give lots of detentions and others give out very few.				
9. When I've done the detention, it removes any bad feelings between me and the teacher.				
10. I'm better behaved for teachers that give out lots of detentions.				

cont.

Tick a box	Strongly Agree	Agree	Disagree	Strongly Disagree
11. Detentions are a good way to make sure our school is a safe school.				
12. What do you think could be done to improve the effectiveness of the detention system?				

Appendix 5
Strategic Planning Template

The following template is a simple grid to help your team create an implementation plan (1–3 years out) for the roll out of RP across the school community. It is part of 'Step 3: Creating a Vision for the Future', in the change process. This is a team activity.

We have created four broad Key Result Areas (KRA's) complete with broad goals:

- Systems

- Learning and Growth

- Resourcing

- Policy.

The results of your audit processes using a SWOT, SOAR or FFA (see Appendix 3) may mean, however, that your broad planning areas are different, and that will be entirely appropriate. You might wish to create a whole page for each area to create more space for your deliberations.

At the top of each page, complete the year, Vision Statement and Key Values (only 3–5, e.g. respect, responsibility, relationships) that underpin the vision as a constant reminder of what is to be achieved. Columns have been created for possible projects, how success will be measured (Measurement), timelines and accountabilities (Person responsible).

Details of each KRA are included in Appendix 6 for your guidance.

Strategic Planning (1–3 years) for the current year, 20____

Vision Statement:

Values: (3–5, e.g. respect, care, student focused, continual improvement…)

Key Result Area (KRA)	Goal	Projects	Measurement	Completion time	Person responsible
Systems	The development of appropriate systems that will reflect RP philosophy, including new understandings of roles and responsibilities, and accountabilities				
Learning and growth	A definition of and outline of necessary development of our people so that their behaviours are consistent with our school values that also underpin RP				
Resourcing	Ensuring that the SLT and Board adapt budgetary plans that allow us to achieve our vision				
Policy	Adaptation/rewriting of policies that are in line with the RP philosophy and our learning and best practice				

Appendix 6
Key Planning Areas

The following key areas are suggestions only, based on the work that schools have discovered for themselves. SWAT or SOAR processes may well reveal other key areas that need equally careful planning.

Key areas listed here are:

- Systems
- Resourcing
- Learning and growth (professional development)
- Policy.

1. Systems

Broadly speaking, the main task with systems is to review and then adapt them to suit the vision for RP. In the first instance, this is usually a review of the disciplinary systems that are in place in the school, for example:

- suspension/fixed-term exclusion/stand-downs
- classroom management strategies
- detentions
- removal from class
- disciplinary flow chart (where are the 'hotspots'?)
- use of community service
- other protocols, including any restorative measures the school might already be using
- pastoral care.

If the school is adopting a relationship-centred approach to all it does, then the review process must ask questions of every protocol and procedure, whether or not it achieves its desired outcomes (and what are they?) and to what extent does the approach work towards the vision of the school and to what extent does it repair, or build or maintain relationships.

This should involve consulting with *all* the major stakeholders of the systems and protocols that are in place. As an example, it would make sense to survey students who may be the 'frequent flyers' of any detention system (see Appendix 4 for a sample survey). It is not good enough to ask *only* staff if any detention system suits *them*. Students must never be excluded from the review process; neither should parents.

Those involved in facilitating the review process should not be surprised if it leads them to thinking through how other systems in the school might be having a positive or unhelpful influence on implementation. We have seen such reviews resulting in adaptation of other systems/protocols such as enrolment, induction, selection and recruitment, human resources and others.

It is critical that SLT and staff are given feedback about what the review identifies and asked for their suggestions; and anything that may be subsequently developed must be in draft form. We suggest a time limit put on any experimental period for trying new ways (e.g. one term, or one semester) before re-engaging with stakeholders.

2. Learning and Growth (Professional Development, PD)

While it is often the case that some teachers have always had values and behaviours that align with the restorative philosophy, bringing *all* the teaching and non-teaching staff and SLT up to speed on the new system protocols and how to use them effectively is ongoing and needs a comprehensive plan. Teachers and others who are taking part in a trial should be prioritised for basic RP training. Keep in mind the student population when you are briefing around any new approaches. Young people will benefit if they understand the rules of engagement – the 'what and why' of what you are trying to achieve.

In other words, don't expect to see what you aren't prepared to first teach.

A range of restorative skills is needed in order to deal with a range of problematic incidents and behaviours across the RP continuum. The following is a list of skills that could be found across and within a restorative school community:

- facilitation of formal conferences, for serious matters
- facilitation of circle processes, class meetings to build and maintain positive classroom relationships
- facilitation of class conferences for situations where classes have become dysfunctional
- mediation and healing circles
- case management of students at risk (development of Individual Management Plans using a restorative approach)
- positive classroom management – basic skills
- social and emotional competency development
- de-escalation
- respectful dialogue at the informal end of the RP spectrum (RP 'chat')
- coaching/mentoring
- leadership development for students and staff in key positions
- staff and student induction
- the range of processes described above being applied to manage staff relationship difficulties.

In fact, anything and everything that can build, maintain and repair relationships needs to be on the list.

Not all classroom teachers would need to be able to facilitate more formal processes, but they at least must be clear about their role as a participant in such formal conferences (being authentic, respectful and honest). They must be adequately skilled to handle the issues that belong with them, so that they can handle their new (old!) responsibilities, instead of referring the issue (usually the student!)

up the line for someone else to deal with. They will also need the basics for developing a healthy, cooperative classroom – relationship management skills.

In the longer term, *leadership development* for middle and senior managers and the implementation team is imperative. This is an area that is often neglected, and a restorative approach will align well with 'relationship-based' leadership.

Staff development activities that have proved effective in bedding down new behaviours and developing distributive leadership include:

- coaching and mentoring

- structured conversations around professional issues – particularly those involving restorative practice so that solutions can be found, rather than people (students and parents) being demonised

- regular meetings (at least fortnightly) between managers and their staff to discuss goals, expectations and modelling of values – constant attention given to 'how we do things around here'. This step becomes critical when a performance conversation has to be initiated, because there is already a relationship of trust that has been developed

- developing relationships 'one conversation at a time' (Scott 2002, p.2)

- development of professional learning communities with like-minded people both within and outside the school

- teaching others the new skills, which cements the skill for the teacher

- encouraging others to be involved in the range of restorative projects that arise as a result of strategic planning.

Induction for new staff should include restorative practice training, and also be extended to relief staff. Both these groups of teachers are the least likely by the sheer nature of the job and/or their newness to develop positive relationships with students quickly, so supporting them with policy and process which values their contributions, and provides them with adequate skills, will be essential. Where possible, include relief staff in professional development opportunities, even if it does mean a day's pay for them to attend.

We strongly recommend that students as part of their induction into a year level are immersed in lessons that actually teach them in explicit ways what the restorative paradigm seeks to achieve and the part they will play in any process, whether as wrongdoer, person harmed, or support person or bystander. In other words, we cannot expect young people to participate in ways that we are not first prepared to teach. Implementation teams (or co-opted sub-committees) will need to take responsibility for putting the curriculum into the form of lesson plans to be delivered appropriate to age levels.

Care needs to be taken around designing PD sessions for the adults in the school community. *Knowledge about adult learning needs and styles would indicate that large groups of people are unlikely to acquire deep skills by attending a one-day course.* What is required is high quality modelling, intense practice *over time*, supported by coaching and problem-solving. Through focus and repetition this leads to new neural pathways in the adult brain, and feedback loops with peers and supervisors/coaches and accountability systems will correct the mistakes we all make when we try something new.

The role of the SLT member on the implementation team becomes critical as they must be prepared to teach, coach and engage other members of the SLT in all of the aspects of the change process and in particular the skills that SLT must now model.

3. Resourcing

For the restorative approach to be taken seriously by all the members of the school community, the implementation, and eventually maintenance, needs to be appropriately resourced. This means that the SLT (and Board/Trustees/Council) needs to adopt a positive attitude to removing any budgetary obstacles (within reason).

At the very least RP needs to be a budget item in the school annual operational plan, approved by the board and be in place for the medium term at least (3–5 years). The implementation team would submit a budget for approval each year. This has implications for strategic planning on a yearly basis.

The sorts of costs that will need a budget are:

- yearly costs for PD (bringing in an 'expert' for in-house workshops/training; sending staff to courses; internal PD)

- operational costs (relieving staff from classes if they are needed to attend formal meetings such as community conferences, class conferences)

- new structures/positions in the school which will enhance the operational protocols – resourcing the work *enough* rather than expecting key staff to do extra work with no relief from timetables

- staff visits to other schools (travel and accommodation)

- sending staff to key professional forums like state, national and international conferences

- costs associated with setting up coaching and performance management systems.

4. Policy

Don't be in a hurry to rewrite your policy. You will need sign off from all stakeholders about what should be included anyway, and that can't happen before some serious education and skilling. Whatever is rewritten will be in draft in the first instance. Reviewing the current school policy can be done about what's working and what isn't, but again we need to be reminded that it's not just about what suits the adults at the school, but what works for the pupils/students and whether or not current policy and practice is *in line with the school vision*. Too often a handful of hard-working staff writes policy and then hopes to see change happen, because words have been committed to paper.

The writing of policy will not create the change. It needs to reflect the philosophy, systems, processes and the learning that any trial has produced. Only then can it be a useful tool to develop and maintain the school's preferred culture. Once there is a well-written policy which indicates what behaviours are expected it can become the pressure on Late Majority adopters to change – for them to realise that the school leadership and governing body are serious now, and they'd better start to get on board. Good policy will also help the school manage performance issues more effectively.

The following is a list of policy 'topics' that might help in framing your policy. It is common for schools to simply copy each other's to save time and effort in the development of their own. Remember, though, what works and is good for one school might not work in another.

Schools that have well-written policies have usually covered the following:

- Vision/mission of the school

- Values/principles/philosophy underpinning the approach

- Rationale, including beliefs about the *purpose* of discipline/ Behaviour Management and what it seeks to achieve in the school community (both learning and personal development)

- Aims of the policy

- Non-negotiables (the right to learn, the right to teach, working together, etc.)

- Expectations regarding behaviours of *all* members of the school community, that is, SLT, staff, students and parents

- Implementation of policy:

  - classrooms

  - playground

  - off-campus (field trips, excursions, sports events)

  - flow chart

  - handling common issues (lateness, uniform, homework, bullying)

- Performance management systems that include information about how staff will be held accountable.

References

Adams, J., Hayes, J., and Hopson, B. (1976) *Transition: Understanding and Managing Personal Change.* London: Martin Robertson.

Ahmed, E., Harris, N., Braithwaite, J. and Braithwaite, V. (2001) *Shame Management Through Reintegration.* Cambridge, UK: Cambridge University Press.

Ahmed, E., Harris, N., Braithwaite, J.B. and Braithwaite, V.A. (eds) (2006) *Shame Management Through Reintegration.* Cambridge: Cambridge University Press.

Arbinger Institute (2006) *The Anatomy of Peace.* Mona Vale, NSW: Woodslane Press.

Australian Broadcasting Commission (2002) Interview by Geraldine Doogue with Louise Porter. ABC Radio National Life Matters. Available at www.abc.net.au/rn/talks/lm/stories/s441942.htm.

Blanchard, K. (2006) *Leading at a Higher Level: Blanchard on Leadership and Creating High Performing Organizations.* New Jersey: Pearson Education.

Blood, P. (2005) *The Australian Context – Restorative Practices as a Platform for Cultural Change in Schools.* Paper presented at the XIV World Congress of Criminology 'Preventing Crime and Promoting Justice: Voices for Change'. Philadelphia, USA, August 7–11, 2005.

Blood, P., and Thorsborne, M. (2005) *The Challenge of Cultural Change: Embedding Restorative Practices in Schools.* Paper presented at Sixth International Conference on Conferencing, Circles and other Restorative Practices: 'Building a Global Alliance for Restorative Practices and Family Empowerment'. Sydney, Australia, March 3–5, 2005.

Blood, P., and Thorsborne, M. (2006) *Overcoming Resistance to Whole-school Uptake of Restorative Practices.* Paper presented at the International Institute of Restorative Practices 'The Next Step: Developing Restorative Communities, Part 2' Conference. Bethlehem, Pennsylvania, USA. 18–20 October 2006.

Blum, R.W., McNeeley, C.A., and Rinehart, P.M. (2002) *Improving the Odds: The Untapped Power of Schools to Improve the Health of Teens.* Minneapolis, MN: Office of Adolescent Health.

Bonnor, C. and Caro, J. (2012) *What Makes a Good School?* Sydney, Australia: New South Publishing.

Braithwaite, J. (2007) *Plenary Address.* Restorative Practices International (RPI), Inaugural Conference 16–19 October, 2007, Best Practice in Restorative Justice 'Transformational Change', Sunshine Coast, QLD, Australia.

Bridges, W. (1995) *Managing Transitions: Making the Most of Change.* Boston, USA: Nicholas Brealey Publishing.

Bridges, W. (2005) *Managing Transitions: Making the Most of Change.* London: Nicholas Brealey Publishing.

Brooks, D. (2012) *The Social Animal.* New York: Random House.

Cameron, L., and Thorsborne, M. (2001) 'Restorative Justice and School Discipline: Mutually Exclusive?' In H. Strang and J. Braithwaite (eds), *Restorative Justice and Civil Society.* Cambridge: Cambridge University Press.

Chan Kim, W., and Mauborgne, R. (2003) 'Tipping point leadership.' *Harvard Business Review*, April 2003, 60–69.

Clarke, R. (1999) *A Primer in Diffusion of Innovations Theory*. Canberra, ACT: Xamax Consultancy. Available at www.anu.edu.au/people/Roger.Clarke/SOS/InnDiff. html, accessed on 19 March 2013.

CASE (Collaborative for Academic, Social, and Emotional Learning) (2011) *What is Social and Emotional Learning (SEL)?* Chicago, IL: CASEL. Available at http://casel. org/why-it-matters/what-is-sel, accessed on 19 March 2013.

Coloroso, B. (2003) *The Bully, the Bullied, and the Bystander: From Pre-school to High School – How Parents and Teachers Can Help Break the Cycle of Violence*. Toronto, ON: HarperCollins.

Corrigan, M. (2009) *Ministry of Education, New Zealand*. Workshop handout.

Dalmau, T. (2000) *The Six Circles Lens*. Dalmau Consulting.

Dalmau, T. (2013) Personal Communication, January 2013.

Doidge, N. (2008) *The Brain that Changes Itself: Stories of Personal Triumph from the Frontiers of Brain Science*. Carlton North, VIC: Scribe Publications.

Egan, G. (1998) *The Skilled Helper: A Problem Management Approach to Helping* (6th edition). Pacific Grove, CA: Brooks/Cole.

Elbertson, N.A., Brackett, M.A., and Weissberg, R.P. (2010) 'School-Based Social and Emotional Learning (SEL) Programming: Current Perspectives.' In A. Hargreaves, A. Lieberman, M. Fullan and D. Hopkins (eds), *Second International Handbook of Educational Change*. New York: Springer.

Ferris, K. (2003) 'Achieving a cultural revolution (1).' *The Journal of the IT Management Forum 2*.

Fullan, M. (2011) *Seminar Series 204: Choosing the Wrong Drivers for Whole System Reform*. Melbourne, VIC: Centre for Strategic Education.

Garner, H. (2004) *Joe Cinque's Consolation: A True Story of Death, Grief and the Law*. Sydney, NSW: Pan MacMillan Australia.

Ghalambor, K. (2011) 'Finding our way: Leadership for an uncertain time by Margaret Wheatley.' *The Evans School Review 1*, 1, 13–16.

Gilligan, J. (1997) *Violence: Reflections on a National Epidemic*. New York: Vintage Books.

Gladwell, M. (2000) *The Tipping Point: How Little Things Can Make a Big Difference*. New York: Little, Brown.

Glaser, D. (1969) *The Effectiveness of a Prison and Parole System*. Indianapolis, IA: Bobbs-Merrill.

Gore, J., Griffiths, T., and Ladwig, J.G. (2004) 'Towards better teaching: Productive pedagogy as a framework for teacher education.' *Teaching and Teacher Education 20*, 375–387.

Government of India (1999) *The Collected Works of Mahatma Gandhi, Vol. 13*. New Delhi: Publications Division, Government of India.

Grange, P. (2013) *The Bluestone Review: A Review of Culture and Leadership in Australian Olympic Swimming*. Abridged version of the Bluestone Review submitted to Swimming Australia on 30 January 2013.

Grille, R. (2005) *Parenting for a Peaceful World*. Alexandria, NSW: Longueville Media.

Harvard University (2012) *Toxic Stress: The Facts*. Cambridge, MA: Center on the Developing Child. Available at http://developingchild.harvard.edu/topics/ science_of_early_childhood/toxic_stress_response, accessed on 20 March 2013.

Heath, C., and Heath, D. (2010) *Switch: How to Change Things When Change Is Hard.* New York: Broadway Books.

Hopkins, B. (2004) *Just Schools: A Whole School Approach to Restorative Justice.* London: Jessica Kingsley Publishers.

Hopkins, B. (2006) *Acting 'Restoratively' and Being 'Restorative' – What Do We Mean? The 'DNA' of Restorative Justice and Restorative Approaches in Schools and Other Institutions and Organisations.* Paper presented at the 4th European Forum for Restorative Justice, Barcelona, June 2006.

Hopkins, B. (2009) *Just Care: Restorative Justice Approaches to Working with Children in Public Care.* London: Jessica Kingsley Publishers.

Hutchison, K. (2006) *Walking After Midnight: One Woman's Journey Through Murder, Justice and Forgiveness.* Vancouver, BC: Raincoast Books.

Illsley Clarke, J., and Dawson, C. (1998) *Growing Up Again: Parenting Ourselves, Parenting Our Children* (2nd edition). Center City, MN: Hazelden.

Johns, B.H., and Carr, V.G. (2002) *Techniques for Managing Verbally and Physically Aggressive Students* (2nd edition). Denver, CO: Love Publishing.

Kelly, V. (2012) *The Art of Intimacy and the Hidden Challenge of Shame.* Maine, USA: Maine Authors Publishing.

Knoster, T., Villa R., and Thousand, J. (2000) 'A Framework for Thinking About Systems Change.' In R. Villa and J. Thousand (eds), *Restructuring for Caring and Effective Education: Piecing the Puzzle Together.* Baltimore: Paul H. Brookes.

Kohn, A. (1996) *Beyond Discipline: From Compliance to Community.* USA: Association for Supervision and Curriculum Development.

Kohn, A. (2000) *The Schools Our Children Deserve: Moving Beyond Traditional Classrooms and 'Tougher Standards'.* New York: Houghton Mifflin.

Kohn, A. (2006) *Beyond Discipline: from Compliance to Community.* Virginia: ASCD.

Kotter, J. (1995) 'Leading change: Why transformation efforts fail.' *Harvard Business Review*, March–April 1995.

Kotter, J. (2007) 'Leading change: Why transformation efforts fail.' *Harvard Business Review*, January 2007.

Kotter, J. (2012) *Step 3: Developing a Change Vision.* Available at www.kotterinternational.com/our-principles/changesteps/step-3, accessed on 20 March 2013.

Kotter, J. (2012a) *Leading Change.* Boston, MA: Harvard Business Review Press.

Kotter, J. (2012b) *Step 4: Communicating the Vision for Buy-in: Ensuring That as Many People as Possible Understand and Accept the Vision.* Available at www.kotterinternational.com/our-principles/changesteps/step-4, accessed on 20 March 2013.

Kotter, J.P., and Cohen, D.S. (2002) *The Heart of Change: Real Life Stories of How People Change Their Organizations.* Boston, MA: Harvard Business Review Press.

Kouzes, J., and Posner, B. (1997) *The Leadership Challenge: How to Keep Getting Extraordinary Things Done in Organisations.* San Francisco: Jossey-Bass.

Lahey, J. (2013) 'Life lessons: Children must be allowed to make mistakes says teacher Jessica Lahey – and a new study details the reasons why.' *The Sydney Morning Herald*, Good Weekend, 23 February 2013.

Lane, R. and Garfield, D. (2012) *Becoming Aware of Feelings: Integration of Cognitive-Developmental, Neuroscientific and Psycholanalytic Perspectives.* Paper presented at Bridging Paradigms: Neuroscience – Emotion – Psychotherapy Conference, George Washington University, Washington, DC, November 2012.

Le Messurier, M. (2010) *Teaching Tough Kids: Simple and Proven Strategies for Student Success.* London: Routledge.

Lee, T. (2004) 'Cultural Change Agent: Leading Transformational Change.' In C. Barker and R. Coy (eds) *The Power of Culture: Driving Today's Organisation.* Sydney, NSW: McGraw Hill.

Lewis, T., Aminia, F., and Lannon, R. (2001) *A General Theory of Love.* New York: Random House.

Lingard, B., Hayes, D., Mills, M., and Christie, P. (2003) *Leading Learning. Making Hope Practical in Schools.* Philadelphia: Open University Press.

Locke, J., Campbell, M.A., and Kavanagh, D.J. (2012) 'Can a parent do too much for their child? An examination by parenting professionals of the concept of overparenting.' *Australian Journal of Guidance and Counselling 22,* 2, 249–265.

MacNeill, N., and Silcox, S. (2003). 'Pedagogic leadership: Putting professional agency back into learning and teaching.' *Curriculum Leadership Journal,* January 2003. Available at www.curriculum.edu.au/leader/pedagogic_leadership:_putting_professional_agency_,4625.html?issueID=9691, accessed on 20 March 2013.

Maines, B., and Robinson, G. (1994) *The No Blame Approach to Bullying.* Paper presented to the British Association for the Advancement of Science 1994 Meeting 'Science in the World Around Us'. Psychology Section – Coping with Challenging Behaviour.

McKenzie, A. (1999) *Transformative Justice – The Brighter Side of Conflict: An Evaluation of School Community Forms in New South Wales Schools.* Paper presented at the Reshaping Australian Institutions Conference 'Restorative Justice and Civil Society', Australian National University, Canberra, February 1999.

Meyer, L.H., and Evans, I.M. (2012) *The Teacher's Guide to Restorative Classroom Discipline.* Thousand Oaks, CA: Corwin Press.

Mezirow, J. (2000) *Learning as Transformation: Critical Perspectives on a Theory in Progress.* San Francisco, CA: Jossey Bass.

Moorhead, G., and Griffin, R.W. (1998) *Managing People and Organizations: Organizational Behavior.* Boston, MA: Houghton Mifflin.

Morrison, B. (2007) *Restoring Safe School Communities: A Whole School Approach to Bullying, Violence and Alienation.* Sydney, NSW: Federation Press.

Morrison, B., Blood, P., and Thorsborne, M. (2005) 'Practicing restorative justice in school communities: addressing the challenge of culture change.' *Public Organization Review: A Global Journal 5,* 4, 335–357.

Moxon, J. (2013) Personal communication regarding 'relational' conversations.

Nathanson, D. (1992) *Shame and Pride: Affect, Sex, and the Birth of the Self.* New York: Norton.

National Academy of Academic Leadership (n.d.) *Leadership and Institutional Change.* Available at www.thenationalacademy.org/ready/change.html, accessed on 25 March 2013.

New South Wales Department of Education and Training (2003) *Quality Teaching in NSW Public Schools.* Sydney, NSW: State of NSW Department of Education and Training Professional Support and Curriculum Development.

Ouchi, W.G. and Jonson, J.B. (1978) 'Types of organizational control and their relationshiop to emotional well being.' *Administrative Science Quarterly 23*, 2, 293–317.

Payne, R. (2009) *A Framework for Understanding Poverty.* Moorabbin, VIC: Hawker Brownlow Education.

Payne, R. (2012) *A Framework for Understanding Poverty.* Moorabbin, VIC: Hawker Brownlow Education. (Revised edition.)

Richmond, C. (2009) *Lead More, Manage Less: Five Essential Behaviour Management Insights for School Leaders.* Gosford, NSW: Scholastic.

Riestenberg, N. (2012) *Circle in the Square. Building Community and Repairing Harm in School.* Minnesota: Living Justice Press.

Rogers, E. (1994) *Diffusion of Innovations and the Mega-Cities Project.* Paper published by the Mega-Cities Project, Publication MCP-011.

Rogers, E. (2003) *Diffusion of Innovation* (5th edition). New York: Free Press.

Sahlberg, P. (2012) *Finnish Lessons: What Can the World Learn from Educational Change in Finland?* Moorabbin, VIC: Hawker Brownlow Education.

Scott, S. (2002) *Fierce Conversations.* London: Piatkis.

Shaw, G., and Wierenga. A (2002) *Restorative Practices Community Conferencing Pilot Evaluation.* Manuscript held at the Faculty of Education, University of Melbourne.

Simpson, S. (2004) 'Unwritten Ground Rules: The Way We Really Do Things Around Here.' In C. Barker and R. Coy (eds) *The Power of Culture: Driving Today's Organisation.* Sydney, NSW: McGraw Hill.

Skiba, R., Simmons, A., Staudinger, L., Rausch, M., Dow, G., and Feggins, R. (2003) *Consistent Removal: Contributions of School Discipline to the School-Prison Pipeline.* Paper presented at the School to Prison Pipeline Conference: Harvard Civil Right Project, May 16–17, 2003.

Taylor, C. (2004) 'The Power of Culture: Turning the Soft Stuff Into Business Advantage.' In C. Barker and R. Coy (eds), *The Power of Culture: Driving Today's Organisation.* Sydney, NSW: McGraw Hill.

Tew, M. (2007) *School Effectiveness: Supporting Success Through Emotional Literacy.* London: Paul Chapman.

Thorsborne, M. (2011) 'Modelling Restorative Practice in the Workplace.' In V. Margraine and A. Macfarlane (eds) *Responsive Pedagogy: Engaging Restoratively with Challenging Behaviour.* Wellington, NZ: NCER.

Virk, M. (2008) *Reena: A Father's Story.* Surrey, BC: Heritage House Publishing.

Wachtel, T. (1999) *Restorative Justice in Everyday Life: Beyond the Formal Ritual.* Paper presented at the Reshaping Australian Institutions Conference: Restorative Justice and Civil Society. The Australian National University, Canberra, 16–18 February 1999.

Wachtel, T., and McCold, P. (2001) 'Restorative Justice in Everyday Life.' In H. Strang and J. Braithwaite (eds) *Restorative Justice and Civil Society.* Cambridge: Cambridge University Press.

Wheatley, M. (1999) 'Bringing Schools Back to Life: Schools as Living Systems.' In F.M. Duffy and J.D. Dale (eds) *Creating Successful School Systems: Voices From the University, the Field and the Community.* Available at www.margaretwheatley.com/articles/lifetoschools.html, accessed on 25 March 2013.

Whitlock, J. (2003) *Fostering School Connectedness. Research Facts and Findings.* New York: ACT for Youth Upstate Center of Excellence, a collaboration of Cornell University, University of Rochester and the New York State Center for School Safety. Available at www.actforyouth.net/resources/rf/rf_connect_1103.pdf, accessed on 25 March 2013.

York Region District School Board (2013) *Positive Climates for Learning.* Available at www.yrdsb.edu.on.ca/pdfs/w/council/PositiveClimateforLearningIntroductory.pdf, accessed on 25 March 2013.

York Region District School Board (2013). Personal Communication, Positive Climates for Learning team.

Zehr, H. (2002) *The Little Book of Restorative Justice.* Intercourse, PA: Good Books.

Zehr, H. (2004) *Plenary Address.* Restorative Justice: New Frontiers Conference, Massey University.

Zehr, H. (2007) *Plenary Address.* Restorative Justice Conference, PD Seminars, Auckland.

Zigarmi, P., and Hoekstra, J. (2006) 'Leading Change.' In K. Blanchard (ed.), *Leading at a Higher Level: Blanchard on Leadership and Creating High Performing Organizations.* Upper Saddle River, NJ: Pearson Education.

Zigarmi, P., Blanchard, K., Zigarmi, D., and Hoekstra, J. (2006) 'Organizational Leadership.' In K. Blanchard (ed.) *Leading at a Higher Level: Blanchard on Leadership and Creating High Performing Organizations.* Upper Saddle River, NJ: Pearson Education.

Zuieback, S. (2012a) *Leadership Practices for Challenging Times: Principles, Skills and Processes That Work.* Ukiah, CA: Synectics, LLC. Available at www.stevezuieback.com/blog/below-the-green-line-theory-to-practice, accessed on 25 March 2013.

Zuieback, S. (2012b) *Below the Green Line – Theory to Practice.* Available at www.stevezuieback.com/blog/below-the-green-line-theory-to-practice/, accessed on 15 January 2013.

Further Reading

About Change

Heath, C., and Heath, D. (2010). *Switch: How to Change Things When Change Is Hard.* New York: Broadway Books.

Kotter, J. (2012) *Leading Change.* Boston: Harvard Business Review Press.

Kotter, J. and Cohen, D. (2005) *My Iceberg is Melting.* New York: St Martin's Press.

Kotter, J. and Rathgeber, H. (2012) *The Heart of Change.* Boston, MA: Harvard Business Review Press.

Stavros, J.M. and Hindrichs, G. (2009) *The Thin Book of SOAR. Building Strengths-Based Strategy.* Bend, OR: Thin Book Publishing.

Wheatley, M. (2006) *Leadership and the New Science: Discovering Order in a Chaotic World.* San Francisco, CA: Berrett Koehler.

Zuieback, S. (2012) *Leadership Practices for Challenging Times.* Ukiah, CA: Synectics LLC.

About Leadership

Kouzes, J., and Posner, B. (1997) *The Leadership Challenge: How to Keep Getting Extraordinary Things Done in Organisations.* San Francisco: Jossey-Bass.

Richmond, C. (2009) *Lead More, Manage Less: Five Essential Behaviour Management Insights for School Leaders.* Gosford, NSW: Scholastic.

Scott, S. (2002) *Fierce Conversations.* London: Piatkis.

Scott, S. (2009) *Fierce Leadership.* New York: Broadway Business.

Zuieback, S. (2012) *Leadership Practices for Challenging Times.* Ukiah, CA: Synectics LLC.

About Restorative Justice

Wormer, S. van, and Walker, L. (eds) (2013) *Restorative Justice Today: Practical Applications.* Thousand Oaks, CA: Sage Publications.

Zehr, H. (1991) *Changing Lenses: New Focus for Crime and Justice.* Harrisonburg, VA: Herald Press.

Zehr, H. (2002) *The Little Book of Restorative Justice.* Intercourse, PA: Good Books.

About Restorative Practice in Schools

Armstrong, M., and Vinegrad, D. (2013) *Working in Circles in Primary and Secondary Classrooms.* Queenscliff, VIC: Inyahead Press.

Hansberry, W. (2009) *Working Restoratively in Schools.* Queenscliff, VIC: Inyahead Press.

Hendry, R. (2009) *Building and Restoring Respectful Relationships in Schools.* London: Routledge.

Hopkins, B. (2004) *Just Schools.* London: Jessica Kingsley Publishers.

Hopkins, B. (2009) *Just Care.* London: Jessica Kingsley Publishers.

Morrison, M. (2007) *Restoring Safe School Communities.* Annandale, NSW: Federation Press.

Riestenberg, N. (2012) *Circle in the Square. Building Community and Repairing Harm in School.* Minnesota: Living Justice Press.

Thorsborne, M. (2012) *A Guide to Workplace Conferencing.* Buderim: Margaret Thorsborne and Associates.

Thorsborne, M., and Vinegrad, D. (2003) *Restorative Practices in Schools. Rethinking Behaviour Management.* Queenscliff, VIC: Inyahead Press.

Thorsborne, M., and Vinegrad, D. (2004) *Restorative Practices in Classrooms. Rethinking Behaviour Management.* Queenscliff, VIC: Inyahead Press.

Thorsborne, M., and Vinegrad, D. (2006) *Restorative Practices and Bullying. Rethinking Behaviour Management.* Queenscliff, VIC: Inyahead Press.

Thorsborne, M., and Vinegrad, D. (2009) *Restorative Justice Pocketbook.* Melbourne, VIC: Teachers' Pocketbooks, Curriculum Press.

About Behaviour Management

Coloroso, B. (2003) *The Bully, the Bullied, and the Bystander: From Pre-school to High School – How Parents and Teachers Can Help Break the Cycle of Violence.* Toronto, ON: HarperCollins.

Frank, L. (2004) *Journey Toward the Caring Classroom: Using Adventure to Create Community in the Classroom.* Bethany, OK: Wood N Barnes.

Hattie, J. (2012) *Visible Learning for Teachers: Maximising Impact on Learning.* London: Routledge.

Kohn, A. (1999) *Punished by Rewards.* Boston: Houghton Mifflin.

Kohn, A. (2006) *Beyond Discipline: from Compliance to Community.* Virginia: ASCD.

Le Messurier, M. (2010) *Teaching Tough Kids: Simple and Proven Strategies for Student Success.* London: Routledge.

Lemov, D. (2010) *Teach Like a Champion.* San Francisco, CA: Jossey-Bass.

Margrain, V., and Macfarlane, A.H. (eds) (2011) *Responsive Pedagogy.* Wellington: NZCER Press.

About Social Emotional Literacy and Pedagogy

Armstrong, M., and Vinegrad, D. (2013) *Working in Circles in Primary and Secondary Classrooms.* Queenscliff, VIC: Inyahead Press.

Payne, R. (1996) *A Framework for Understanding Poverty.* Highlands, TX: Aha! Process Inc.

Roffey, S. (2006) *Circle Time for Emotional Literacy.* London: Paul Chapman.

Sahlberg, P. (2012) *Finnish Lessons.* Melbourne, VIC: Hawker Brownlow Education.

About Neuroscience and Human Development

Brooks, D. (2011) *The Social Animal.* New York: Random House.

Doidge, N. (2008) *The Brain that Changes Itself.* Melbourne, VIC: Scribe.

Grille, R. (2005) *Parenting for a Peaceful World.* Woollahra, NSW: Longueville Media.

Holinger, P. (2003) *What Babies Say Before They Can Talk.* New York: Simon and Schuster.

Kelly, V. (2012) *The Art of Intimacy and the Hidden Challenge of Shame.* Maine, USA: Maine Authors Publishing.

Lewis, T., Amini, F., and Lannon, R. (2001) *A General Theory of Love.* New York: Vintage Books.

Nathanson, D. (1992) *Shame and Pride: Affect, Sex, and the Birth of Self.* New York: Norton.

Some Websites

General information

Restorative Justice Online
www.restorativejustice.org

Centre for Restorative Justice
www.sfu.ca/crj

Justiceworks Ltd
www.justiceworksltd.org

The Aims of Restorative Justice
www.beyondintractability.org/essay/restorative_justice

Restorative Justice Council
www.restorativejustice.org.uk

International Institute for Restorative Practices
www.iirp.org
www.cehd.umn.edu/ssw/rjp

RP for Schools
www.rpforschools.net

Resources developed by education departments

New Zealand
www.vln.school.nz/vln_google_search?q=restorative%20practice

Minnesota (USA)
http://education.state.mn.us/MDE/StuSuc/SafeSch/RestorMeas/index.html

Subject Index

Author Index